Robert Gnuse

THE AUTHORITY
OF THE BIBLE

Theories of Inspiration, Revelation
and the Canon of Scripture

Paulist Press ● *New York/Mahwah*

Library of Congress
Catalog Card Number: 84-62562

ISBN: 0-8091-2692-3

Published by Paulist Press
997 Macarthur Boulevard
Mahwah, N.J. 07430

Printed and bound in the United States of America

CONTENTS

iii

To
Elizabeth Hammond Gnuse

Chapter One

INTRODUCTION

All Christendom affirms that the Bible has authority for the Church, but beyond that consensus denominations and theologians move in radically diverse directions. This book shall investigate and evaluate those directions to obtain sensitivity for the complexity of the problem. Our purpose is not to offer profound new insights or say anything that has not been said before. This text is merely an introduction to the diversity of those opinions. It has as its chief goal the task of organizing those opinions into a logical classification for the interested reader and the student of Scripture.

When asked about the authority of the Bible the average Christian would probably respond with some reference to the concept of inspiration. Throughout much of the Church's history biblical inspiration has been connected with the concept of biblical authority, sometimes even directly equated. A primary purpose of this book is to show that other ways of understanding the Bible's authority have been proposed, and some of them have distinct advantages over inspiration models. Hopefully, the reader will be led to realize that different models have been proposed by theologians to describe the authority of Scripture, and each of them has strengths and weaknesses.

Thomas Hoffman wrote an essay on the nature of inspiration and its relation to Scriptural authority. He noted that inspiration, normativeness, and canonicity are three different issues in the discussion of Scripture. This work will affirm his observations. According to his evaluation inspiration becomes a vague category to use in describing the authority of the Bible when it is confused with those other concepts. Hopefully, this work will separate and evaluate the different concepts involved in the question of biblical authority. Finally, Hoffman lamented the lack of discussion undertaken outside of Protestant evangelical circles, especially among Roman Catholics, concerning the issue of inspiration, canon, and authority. This work is a small attempt to fill that void.[1]

Three questions must be raised concerning the authority of the Bible: (1) What do we mean by the word authority? (2) Why is the Bible authoritative? (3) How is this authority of the Bible applied to the faith and practice of the Church? We shall consider the second question—the reasons for which the Bible is said to have authority. The first question cannot be treated in detail here, for it involves far more than the biblical discipline. The third question concerning the application of authority to the life and practice of the Church would involve a tedious consideration of how various texts have been applied at various times to Church life, from Communion practice to the wearing of hats. Discussion of this question would entail determining what is legitimately authoritative for the life of the Church and how it should be translated from the cultural categories of the biblical period to our present age.[2] That, too, is beyond the capacity of our study.

The basic definition of authority is to speak of that "which is acknowledged as rightly and worthily commanding loyalty and obedience."[3] Authority should provide a sense of identity, a feeling of hope, standards for belief and behavior, and guidelines by which we compare ourselves to these norms. For the Christian the Bible meets these norms effectively, but it does not meet them completely. The Church must develop additional institutions, such as preaching, teaching, and counseling roles, in order to effectively implement the authority of Scripture. Though the Bible is authoritative for theology and Church practice, it is inert, and it must be activated in the life and institutions of the Church.[4]

1. Thomas Hoffman, "Inspiration, Normativeness, Canonicity, and the Unique Character of the Bible," *Catholic Biblical Quarterly* 44 (1982): 447–469.

2. This question is addressed by several essays in a work edited by Frederick Greenspahn, *Scripture in the Jewish and Christian Traditions: Authority, Interpretation, Relevance* (Nashville: Abingdon, 1982), including Sheldon Blank, "The Hebrew Scriptures as a Source for Moral Guidance," pp. 168–182; Richard McBrien, "Catholicism as an Integrationist Perspective," pp. 183–200; and Krister Stendahl, "Ancient Scripture in the Modern World," pp. 201–214.

3. Robert Bryant, *The Bible's Authority Today* (Minneapolis: Augsburg, 1968), p. 156.

4. William Countryman, *Biblical Authority or Biblical Tyranny?* (Philadelphia: Fortress, 1981), p. 31; David Kelsey, *The Uses of Scripture in Recent Theology* (Philadelphia: Fortress, 1975), p. 94.

Scripture is authoritative for the Church because of what it does for the Christian community, not because of an inherent quality. To call literature or ancient texts ''Christian Scripture'' means that they are used in the life of the Church to direct the community's faith, moral direction, theological expression, and religious customs. They are used to create and preserve the self-identity of the community of faith.[5]

The variety of ways in which Scripture is used in Church life by different theologians and Church denominations indicates that the concept of biblical authority does not entail any one method. A plurality of methods have been used consciously and unconsciously in the Church. When theologians use Scripture as an authority, they really have an aspect of Scripture or a particular perspective by which they interpret the whole Bible.[6]

Each theologian uses a particular pattern by which he or she reorganizes the biblical data in systematic fashion. Kelsey calls such a pattern for perceiving Scripture a ''discrimen'' or a ''configuration of certain criteria.''[7] This configuration is determined by the faith of the interpreter and includes those ideas which summarize the Christian faith for that individual. The interpreter or theologian does not really translate the meaning of the Bible into the modern idiom. Rather, the theologian uses the discrimen or pattern to draw forth a message from the biblical text and put it into the culture, world view, and religious tradition of the audience which he or she addresses. In one sense this discrimen is the true authoritative principle for each theologian.[8] Nonetheless, the theologian may appeal to a particular model of authority.

The various models used by theologians have been classified by this work into five categories: (1) inspiration, (2) salvation history, (3) existential, (4) Christocentric, and (5) models of limited authority. Each of these categories has been subdivided, as will be evident upon reading each chapter. Inspiration receives the most extensive treatment, for it has received the greatest attention in the greater Christian tradition.

These categories are arbitrary creations by this author. For the sake of pedagogy generalizations have to be made in order to present the in-

---

5. Kelsey, *Scripture,* pp. 89–94.
6. Ibid., pp. 101–103, 143.
7. Ibid., pp. 101–103, 159–170.
8. Ibid., pp. 182–201.

formation in manageable fashion. Not everyone will agree with all the distinctions or classifications of particular individuals. The arbitrary nature of the scheme becomes evident when certain significant theologians (i.e., Karl Barth) appear in more than one category. If the reader wishes to relocate any given individual, the character of the categories will not be vitiated. A fuller or more sophisticated study would blur the distinctions and speak of a more fluid spectrum of opinions. Ultimately the view of every theologian is unique, and justice would demand a separate category for each. Such is a task fit only for Sisyphus.

Other scholars have made attempts at classifying the different models of authority, and the student would do well to consider some of these evaluations also. Their classifications indicate the variety of approaches which are possible in seeking to evaluate the material.

A very well developed theological assessment of different authority models is provided by David Kelsey in *The Uses of Scripture in Recent Theology*. Kelsey does not attempt a complete typology; rather he selects significant individuals as paradigms of particular approaches. The various models or case studies he evaluates include: (1) "patterns of logical connections among concepts" (Hans Werner Bartsch), (2) "patterns of doctrinal arguments" (Benjamin Warfield), (3) "patterns giving the structure to a substantial stretch of world history" (George Ernest Wright), (4) "patterns in narrated sequences of intentions and actions" (Karl Barth), (5) "patterns of biblical images" (Lionel Thorton), (6) "patterns of biblical religious symbols" (Paul Tillich), and (7) "patterns of kerygmatic statements" (Rudolf Bultmann).[9]

Markus Barth also provides a number of models for understanding the authority of the Bible. He perceives the following categories: (1) the Bible as sacred literature, (2) the humanistic or philological argument (written literature should be the foundation for a high religion), (3) the Bible as a norm or law, (4) philosophical argument (the Bible as a source for a formal principle), (5) pragmatic argument (the Bible has authority

---

9. Ibid., pp. 14–88. In another work Kelsey provides categories for interpretative models which parallel this author's format: (1) history as sacred history, subdivided into conservative and evangelical/pietistic models, (2) history as a critical reconstruction, subdivided into liberal nineteenth century Protestant and existential twentieth century Protestant models, and (3) history as narrative, "Protestant Attitudes Regarding Methods of Biblical Interpretation," *Jewish and Christian Traditions*, pp. 151–161.

because the Church grants it), and (6) Christological (the Bible testifies to Christ).[10] Like Kelsey he does not attempt a typology of theologians.

A different approach is undertaken by David Bartlett who seeks to evaluate the authority behind the various types of literature found in the Bible. In particular, he evaluates: (1) words of God, especially those mediated by the prophets in the Old Testament and the Gospel narratives, (2) historical narrative, especially the events in the Old Testament and the Gospel narratives, (3) wisdom literature, both the Old Testament wisdom books and the proverbial sayings of Jesus and Paul, and (4) witness literature, the personal confessions of individuals like Jeremiah and Paul.[11] His assessment is very helpful and functions in complementary fashion to this work. His categories differ from what this work proposes, for herein we shall offer a typology of different theological positions rather than evaluating the genres of biblical literature.

Though it is similar in function to the work of Kelsey and Barth, this work is not as theologically profound in its analysis. Rather, it tries to be more comprehensive in scope and easier to read for the interested student.

A final word of clarification is necessary. The words "Scripture" and "Bible" are used interchangeably. The word "canon" is basically synonymous with these two words, but it denotes more properly the official corpus of literature designated by the Church for theological use in the fourth century A.D. The word "canon" used here has a certain formal nuance; it refers to the end product of a dynamic tradition making process.

---

10. Markus Barth, "Sola Scriptura," *Scripture and Ecumenism,* ed. Leonard Swidler, Duquesne Studies, Theological Studies, Vol. 3 (Pittsburgh: Duquesne, 1965), pp. 86–92.

11. David Bartlett, *The Shape of Scriptural Authority* (Philadelphia: Fortress, 1983), pp. 11–130.

Chapter Two

HISTORICAL PRELUDE

Throughout history the Bible has exerted influence on the development of Christian art, literature, conscience, and, in particular, theology. From the beginning the Church sensed that whatever created the Scripture had given birth to the Church, and a certain spiritual inspiration and direction resided within the covers of the text.[1] Most references in the pre-modern Church Fathers speak of the inspiration of Scripture in a general way as an underlying testimony to its binding authority.

Pre-Modern Period

The pre-modern Church and its theologians did not hold to a naive or simplistic view of biblical authority. Inspiration was the most common model used by patristic, medieval, and early modern theologians, but one may perceive that individual theologians often struggled to clarify the concept of inspiration in a sophisticated fashion. Debate existed as to whether the words of the Bible were to be viewed as divine dictation or a divine expression through the medium of human finitude. Theologians often preferred to speak of divine "accommodation" or "condescension" in the words of Scripture.[2] A transcendent deity who addressed humanity through human words must work with the limitations of human minds and language. The human side of the text was recognized to some degree by many of the Church Fathers. At times a critical exegesis could

---

1. Charles Harold Dodd, *The Authority of the Bible*, rev. ed. (London: Fontana, 1960), p. 187.
2. Bruce Vawter, *Biblical Inspiration*, Theological Resources (Philadelphia: Westminster, 1972), pp. 40–57.

proceed which acknowledged the limitations of the scientific and cultural perspectives of the biblical text. In the early modern period Luther and Calvin, who both held a high view of Scripture's authority, could make very critical observations about parts of the text.

Even though the extent and nature of inspiration was not totally clarified, nevertheless, prior to the modern period the authority of the Bible was assumed in some form by everyone. Not until after the Protestant Reformation would the question of authority become a problematic issue.

With the Reformation in the sixteenth century the Protestant insistence upon "sola scriptura" for doing theology was an attempt to replace tradition, philosophy, and ecclesiastical structures with the authority of the biblical text. Authority once vested in Church structures was now laid completely on the Bible.[3] Among Protestants this led to an increased reverence for the text which viewed it as a compendium of fixed theological statements by the age of orthodoxy in the seventeenth century.

Roman Catholic polemics against the Protestants often sought to undermine the authority of Scripture in favor of the authority of the Church. Individual theologians produced models for understanding inspiration and authority which limited the extent of divine authority behind the text; hence, they were called minimalists. Sixtus of Sienna (1575) felt that the Scriptures were authoritative merely because the Church subsequently approved them after their creation. Leonard Lessius (1587) said that the human writings of Scripture were subsequently approved by the Holy Spirit. Lessius, Francisco Suarez (1599–1628), Jacques Bonfrere (1625), Richard Simon (1680), and Vincent Conteson (1681) suggested that God provided negative assistance only to help the writers avoid errors in the text.[4] This latter view of divine assistance against errors was revived in the modern period by Johann Jahn (1802), Jan Herman Janssens (1818), and Franz Heinrich Reusch (1870). Daniel Bonifacius Haneberg (1850)

---

3. Dodd, *Authority,* p. 20; Hans Joachim Kraus, *Geschichte der historisch-kritischen Erforschung des Alten Testaments,* 2nd ed. (Neukirchen-Vluyn: Neukirchener, 1969), pp. 6–38; and Karl Rahner, *Inspiration in the Bible,* 2nd ed., trans. Charles Henkey, Questiones disputatae, Vol. 1 (New York: Herder and Herder, 1964), p. 32.

4. John McKenzie, "Inspiration," *Dictionary of the Bible* (New York: Macmillan, 1965), p. 391; Richard Smith, "Inspiration and Inerrancy," *The Jerome Biblical Commentary,* eds. Raymond Brown, Joseph Fitzmyer, and Roland Murphy (Englewood Cliffs: Prentice-Hall, 1968), p. 505; James Tunstead Burtchaell, *Catholic Theories of Biblical Inspiration Since 1810: A Review and Critique* (Cambridge, England: University Press, 1969), pp. 44–49, 54–55; and Vawter, *Inspiration,* pp. 63–68.

revived the concept of subsequent approval by the Church.[5] Both minimalist positions were condemned by Vatican I.

The minimalist position which may have originated as a polemic against Protestants actually lies outside the mainstream of Roman Catholic thought. A number of theologians defended what can be termed as the maximalist position, a view which attributes a high view of inspiration (at times even dictation) to all of the biblical text. Such advocates included Henry of Ghent (1276–1292), Melchior Cano (1585), Domingo Bañez (1585), Gregario di Valencia (1591), and Charles Rene Billuart (1758).[6]

The traditional and official position of the Roman Catholic Church was stated at Trent (1545–1563). On the question of biblical authority and its relation to tradition the Council of Trent was not too dissimilar to Protestant definitions, despite the old stereotype that Protestants affirm only Scripture while Roman Catholics use the two sources of Scripture and tradition for doing theology. The Tridentine definition views Scripture as the *norma normans et non normata* or "the norm which governs but is not governed." Scripture is thus seen as the norm for the traditions of the Church. Among Lutherans, as representative of one form of Protestantism, the Book of Concord views Scripture as *norma normans* or the "norm which governs," and the traditions or the confessions constitute the *norma normata,* "the norm which is governed," and it is governed by Scripture. Despite their attempts to dispute with the Protestants, Roman Catholics were closer on this issue than they would admit. However, the differences which might arise among individual theologians could be great. For that matter, the divisions within a denomination, such as the gap between minimalists and maximalists, could be greater than the so-called chasm between denominations.

MODERN PERIOD

With the rise of modern empirical sciences and the creation of a new world view the authority of the Bible seemed to be challenged. The crisis was acute for Protestants who had invested so much in the Scripture principle. After the peak of Orthodoxy around 1700 the historian begins to

---

5. J. McKenzie, "Inspiration," p. 391; Smith, "Inspiration," p. 505; Burtchaell, *Catholic Theories,* pp. 50–52, 56; and Vawter, *Inspiration,* pp. 68–70.

6. Smith, "Inspiration," p. 505; and Vawter, *Inspiration,* pp. 58–63, 73–75.

notice a rapid decline in the quality of orthodox theology and an increasing defensiveness on the issue of Scripture and its authority.

By the nineteenth century the best minds of Protestant Europe had turned their backs on the old orthodoxy for a new liberal theology which did not affirm the concept of biblical authority. Led by the theology of Friedrich Schleiermacher a new age of theology had begun. Only in conservative confessional circles in Europe and in American Protestant denominations did the old orthodoxy with its high view of biblical authority and strict concept of inspiration persist.

The nineteenth century also saw the beginnings of a new biblical criticism. New Testament critical methodologies were pioneered by the Tübingen school, and new insights concerning the development of the Old Testament finally culminated in the grand scheme of Julius Wellhausen. Though the early architects of biblical criticism were far more extreme than their twentieth century counterparts, the demise of the orthodox view of biblical authority and strict inspiration seemed assured.[7]

With the rise of modern empirical sciences outside the Church and biblical criticism inside the Church the high degree of authority invested by Protestants in the Bible seemed threatened. Debate arose and clarification was necessary. Though at first Protestants were threatened by this development and sought to redefine or buttress the authority of Scripture, the questions eventually came to Roman Catholic circles in the Modernist controversy.

Discussion concerning the nature of biblical inspiration blossomed in the nineteenth century for Roman Catholics.[8] A number of theologians proposed that only portions of Scripture were inspired, and thus those parts which might disagree with modern understandings would offer no offense, since they were part of the biblical writer's limited world view. Advocates of this position, which is called "content inspiration" (*realinspiration* in German and *res et sententiae* in Latin) included Johannes

---

7. Alan Richardson, "The Rise of Modern Biblical Scholarship and Recent Discussion of the Authority of the Bible," *The Cambridge History of the Bible*, Vol. 3: *The West from the Reformation to the Present Day*, ed. Stanley Greenslade (Cambridge, England: University Press, 1963), pp. 294–296.

8. Burtchaell, *Catholic Theories*, pp. 58–163 et passim, offers the best and fullest exposition of the views presented by these individual scholars; and Terence Forestell, "Bible, II (Inspiration)," *New Catholic Encyclopedia*, 17 vols. (New York: McGraw-Hill, 1967), 2:381–386.

Perrone (1835–1842), Johann Scholz (1845), Franciscus Patritius (1851), Joseph Kleutgen (1867), August Rohling (1872), Johannes Franzelin (1875), Hugo Hurter (1876), Thomas Lamy (1877), Franz Hettinger (1879), Francois Lenormant (1880–1884), Franciscus Schmid (1885), Salvatore di Bartolo (1888–1889), Peter Dausch (1891), Paul Schanz (1892–1904), Christian Pesch (1894–1906), and the most well-known of all, Cardinal John Henry Newman. The majority of these scholars were Jesuits, and the position almost became the formal view of the order. In opposition to their position a number of other theologians articulated a fuller concept of verbal inspiration. This model was advocated by Dominicans and built upon Thomistic thought. This new verbal inspiration was a modern theory which spoke of God as the primary author and the human writer was the secondary author or instrumental cause. Advocates included Heinrich Denzinger (1857), Herman Schell (1889–1893), Thomas-Marie Pegues (1895), Domenico Zanecchia (1898), Marie-Joseph Lagrange (1895–1905), Constantin Chavin (1896), Ludovicus Billot (1906), William Barry (1906), Thomas Calmes (1907), and Jean Baivel (1910). The position of "idea inspiration" was predominant at the time of Vatican I (1870). But after Leo XIII called for a revival of Thomistic studies, the position of verbal inspiration and its leading defender, Marie-Joseph Lagrange, was in ascendancy (1893–1907). Unfortunately the Modernist controversy cast a pall of suspicion over everyone after 1907, and the positions of both parties waned in the ensuing years.[9]

The discussion of inspiration and authority led the Roman Catholic Church to clarify its position. The two ideologies which struggled for the mind of the Church were the position associated with Cardinal Franzelin (the inspiration of words and ideas) and the position later associated with Marie-Joseph Lagrange (instrumentality or verbal inspiration). The former appealed to theologians and the latter appealed to biblical exegetes.

Vatican Council I (1870) was a vindication of Cardinal Franzelin's position over the limited views of inspiration offered by Johann Jahn ("negative assistance") and Daniel Haneberg ("subsequent approval"). Inspiration was conceived as a positive influence upon the sacred writers by God as to render him the true author of the biblical text. The Council

---

9. Burtchaell, *Catholic Theories*, pp. 58–163.

also affirmed that Scripture and tradition were not two separate sources.[10]

The encyclical of Leo XIII entitled *Providentissimus Deus* (1893) caused the discussion to move in the direction of the Lagrange position. Leo spoke of the writers of the Bible as individuals who "correctly conceived, accurately wrote down and truthfully expressed all that he intended."[11] The position of verbal inspiration was more compatible with this encyclical, and its use of Thomistic categories brought it into favor. For Lagrange God was the principal cause who elevated the natural abilities of the human author, or instrumental cause, to write material that was both human in origin and divine by inspiration.[12] The theory sounded traditional in that both the words and ideas were viewed as inspired, but the human side of the Bible was not forgotten as it had been in the old dictation theories.

The Modernist controversy brought discredit to all parties involved. Those scholars who were condemned most readily were the ones who had expressly admitted the presence of errors in the text. Their view of verbal inspiration could have been conceivably more conservative than the "inspiration of ideas" position of Franzelin and others, but their willingness to speak of relative truth or even errors brought condemnation. This position of inspiration without inerrancy (comparable to Protestants today who advocate infallibility without inerrancy) included advocates like Richard Simpson (1850), Friedrich von Hügel (1894–1895), Jules Didiot (1891), F. Girerd (1903–1905), Franz von Hummelauer (1904), and most notably Alfred Loisy (1901–1908). The Modernist controversy did not bring formal condemnation to the position of Lagrange, but defenders of this viewpoint fell silent. The encyclical of Pius X entitled *Pascendi Dominici Gregis* (1907) and the later encyclical of Benedict XV, *Spiritus Paraclitus* (1920), condemned any view of inspiration with limited inerrancy

---

10. Pierre Benoit, "Inspiration and Revelation," *The Human Reality of Sacred Scripture,* Concilium, Vol. 10 (New York: Paulist, 1965), p. 8; Derek Holmes and Robert Murray, eds., *On the Inspiration of Scripture* by John Henry Newman (Washington: Corpus, 1966), pp. 52–59, point out that Cardinal Johannes Franzelin moderated between the ideas of negative assistance and divine dictation by stating that God gave ideas, men gave the words, but God preserved the words from any error (*De divina Traditione et Scriptura*— 1870), a view later characterized by Lagrange as psychological vivisection; and Burtchaell, *Catholic Theories,* p. 283.

11. J. McKenzie, "Inspiration," p. 390.

12. Ibid., pp. 391–392.

or which spoke of relative truth, as did Hummelauer.[13] Exegetical discussion on inspiration was ended.

The middle of the twentieth century saw a reversal of this stringent position. In 1943 Pius XII issued the more favorable encyclical *Divino Afflante Spiritu* which accepted the use of critical biblical methodologies. The age of Roman Catholic biblical scholarship had begun. The document *Verbum Dei* (Constitution on Divine Revelation) issued by Vatican II has furthered this impetus. Several revisions during the Second Vatican Council between 1962 and 1964 transformed it from a narrow statement to a more open definition, which could admit the truth of salvation was without error while the written words need not be.[14] A number of the delegates at the Council were uncomfortable with the concept of inerrancy (Cardinals Meyer, König, Simons, and Fathers Leger, Jäger, and Weber), and so the concept of inerrancy found in the early drafts was replaced by statements which defined truth in terms of the plan of salvation.[15] The final statement read, ". . . we must profess of the books of Scripture that they teach with certainty, with fidelity and without error the truth which God wanted recorded in the sacred writings for the sake of our salvation."[16]

Thus the Roman Catholic Church has rejected several views in the last two centuries: subsequent approval by the Church or the Spirit, negative assistance by the Spirit, verbal dictation, inspiration of ideas, inspiration of faith and morals, and total inerrancy. But all of these pertain only to the matter of inspiration. Inspiration may not be the important facet in understanding the authority of the Bible. If inspiration is the reason for accepting biblical authority, then the issue is resolved, but if the authority of the Bible is located in a cause other than inspiration, then the discussion has only begun for Roman Catholics.

Roman Catholics and Protestants now stand at the same juncture. The Bible is recognized by all as having authority, but the extent of the authority lacks consensus. We sense it to be an historically bound doc-

13. Burtchaell, *Catholic Theories*, pp. 164–229, 232–233; and Dewey Beegle, *Scripture, Tradition, and Infallibility* (Grand Rapids: Eerdmans, 1973), p. 147.

14. Vawter, *Inspiration*, pp. 70–71, 143–150.

15. Burtchaell, *Catholic Theories*, p. 268; John Scullion, *The Theology of Inspiration*, Theology Today, Vol. 10 (Notre Dame: Fides, 1970), pp. 86–88; and Vawter, *Inspiration*, pp. 143–150.

16. Karl Rahner, *Foundations of Christian Faith*, trans. William Dych (New York: Seabury, 1978), p. 375.

ument which spoke authoritative words to a former people. These words seem authoritative to us at times, and at times they appear outdated and irrelevant. The Bible is clearly a source to what the faith historically was, and in some form it may be a source or guide to what the faith should be today.[17]

We need to turn our study to a consideration of the different models for understanding the authority of the Bible. Which of them can best offer us a rationale for understanding the Bible's authority for use in the Church today?

---

17. John Bright, *The Authority of the Old Testament* (Grand Rapids: Baker, 1967), pp. 28–29, 143.

Chapter Three

INSPIRATION AS A GENERAL MODEL FOR AUTHORITY

The most frequently used model for affirming the authority of Scripture is to stress its inspiration by God. The reason lies in the ultimate authority of God, for if Scripture is seen as something given by God to humanity, then it must partake of his ultimate divine nature.

Though direct testimony in the Bible to the function of inspiration is not frequent, the idea was seized upon by theologians in the Church and developed as an argument for accepting the Bible as authoritative for faith and practice. Passages in 2 Timothy 3:16 ("all Scripture is given by inspiration of God"), 2 Peter 1:20–21 ("Holy men of God spoke as they were moved by the Holy Spirit"), John 10:35 ("Scripture cannot be broken"), and others were cited to prove that God was the author of the Bible by the process of inspiring or breathing into the writers the divine message.

Since this divine-human relationship is not explained by the text, great debate has arisen over the extent of the divine or human origin of the text. The Church has always believed in inspiration, but the idea has never been clearly defined in authoritative fashion for the consensus of the Church. Conservative Protestants and Catholic maximalists affirm the priority of divine authorship, and liberal Protestants and Catholic minimalists point out the human origins and limitations. In addition, there seems to be an unconscious presupposition among many theologians that the authors of Scripture spoke with profound wisdom that even they did not comprehend. The message had a fuller sense or meaning that would unfold in the development of the later biblical tradition and the exegesis of the Christian Church. Thus an almost magical quality was imparted to the words. Since no one truly understands the dynamic of inspiration, a wide range of opinion has developed on the subject.[1]

INSPIRATION IN THE BIBLICAL TEXT

At first glance there appear to be frequent references to inspiration in the Bible. However, closer consideration reveals that only a few are germane to the study of inspiration as we understand it.

In the Old Testament the concept of spirit possession is frequently mentioned. Warriors are seized by the spirit of the Lord and go forth to fight battles for the people of Israel. Numerous examples can be found in the Books of Judges and 1 Samuel. But this is hardly inspiration! Nonetheless, many theologians fit these texts into the large category of inspiration in order to lend greater weight to the biblical testimony on the subject.

The spirit possession of the prophets is more appropriate for consideration. Prophets are seized by the spirit of the Lord and utter his words (Num 22:38, 2 Sam 23:2, Hos 9:7, Ez 11:5, Is 59:21, and elsewhere). At times this spirit possession can be ecstatic and lead the prophets to do wild things (1 Sam 10:10–13; 19:20–24), nor does this spirit always bring the truth (1 Kgs 22:19–23). Such phenomena discomfort the traditional Christian concept of inspiration.

The prophets frequently utter the expression, ''Thus says the Lord,'' as an introduction to prophetic oracles. Such texts are quoted by theologians to affirm inspiration, and usually advocates of strict inspiration theories appeal heavily to them. For the expression implies that the prophet is quoting the words given directly to him by God. But the formula appears to be a literary convention taken over by the prophets from the language of ancient Near Eastern diplomatic activity. The ancient messenger used such a formula to preface the message in order to assure diplomatic immunity from a potentially angry recipient of a bad message.[2] In this regard, the frequent proclamation of judgment oracles by

---

1. Dennis Eric Nineham, ''Wherein Lies the Authority of the Bible?'' *On the Authority of the Bible: Some Recent Studies* (London: SPCK, 1960), p. 88; and Avery Dulles, ''The Authority of Scripture: A Catholic Perspective,'' *Jewish and Christian Traditions,* p. 29.

2. Claus Westermann, *Basic Forms of Prophetic Speech,* trans. Hugh White (Philadelphia: Westminster, 1967), pp. 98–128.

the prophets made it wise for them to use a similar formula to safeguard themselves from a hostile crowd reaction (for example, in Jeremiah 26:1–24 this concept enabled Jeremiah to escape with his life). The prophet used the formula to tell the people that the word or judgment came from Yahweh and not the prophet's own personal opinions. The formula also functioned dramatically to get the attention of the audience. The formula, "Thus says the Lord," is not a description of the process of inspiration, but rather a literary convention used by the prophets.

An additional oversight is made by those who appeal to this formula to support a belief in strict inspiration. The prophets did not write; they were oral spokespersons or preachers to their society. The word of the Lord for them was an oral message, not a written word. Inspiration theories often overlook this, and proceed to quote the Old Testament passages in reference to Scripture in its written form. The distinction between the dynamic oral message and the later written form is blurred by this appeal, sometimes deliberately.

A closer look at Old Testament prophecy reveals a different process than is commonly assumed. Prophets were not automatons of God. They were dynamic spokespersons who articulated the divine message in their own words. The experience of the divine was inexpressible but real for them. The articulation of the message was in their own words. The prophetic mode of inspiration was a dynamic process of cooperation between God and prophet. Prophets, like Jeremiah, could dialogue and even argue with God. The relationship was one of personal communion, and Isaiah could speak of even being in God's divine council. God provided the impulse to speak and the prophets provided the language, as 2 Peter 1:20–21 clearly affirms. Their inspiration is far more dynamic and has more human dimension than is frequently realized.[3]

The Christian concept of inspiration is not really found in the Old Testament. At best one could say that Old Testament ideas would evolve and provide input for the New Testament. Within the context of Old Testament theology inspiration does not really play an important role. The

---

3. Gerhard von Rad, *The Message of the Prophets*, trans. David Stalker (New York: Harper and Row, 1967), pp. 30–76; Robert Scott, *Relevance of the Prophets* (New York: Macmillan, 1968), pp. 90–113; Vawter, *Inspiration*, pp. 8–19; and Johannes Lindblom, *Prophecy in Ancient Israel* (Philadelphia: Fortress, 1973), pp. 105–219.

concept is really developed in the later stages of New Testament writings.[4]

Before arriving at the New Testament understanding mention must be made of another source of input for the Christian concept of inspiration. The Greeks had a concept of mantic inspiration which perceived that the prophet was seized by a *daimon* or the deity and forced to utter words in a frenzied state which came directly from the divine source. In this condition the mind of the prophet might even be unconscious; so possessed by the *daimon* was the seer that he or she might not remember the oracle when it was finished. This Greek view was mediated to the Jewish tradition in diaspora and was part of the heritage for later Christians and Jews. The famous Jewish theologian Philo is usually credited for introducing this "mantic" view of prophecy. The prophet was not seen to be in a personal relationship with the deity, as Old Testament prophets had been; rather he or she was merely a tool by which the deity communicated.[5]

The New Testament inherited both the dynamic view of inspiration from Old Testament prophecy and the mantic view of the Greeks, but the former understanding predominated. Jesus was not as mechanical in his understanding as was Philo. The Spirit inspired David, but David spoke the words; and the human side of the process was emphasized in the discussion of Moses' bill of divorce in Deuteronomy.[6] These remarks in the sayings of Jesus reflect an attitude toward inspiration which pervades the rest of the New Testament.

Inspiration is directly discussed only in the later New Testament writings. Unfortunately, dogmatic understandings of Scripture too often prevent the exegete from properly evaluating the texts in context. The passages which speak of inspiration refer most evidently to the Old Testament writings as being inspired, though that literature was not yet in a unified canonical form. The understanding of inspiration is comparable

---

4. J. McKenzie, *A Theology of the Old Testament* (Garden City: Doubleday, 1976), p. 133.

5. Smith, "Inspiration," p. 503; Beegle, *Scripture,* pp. 126–132; and Vawter, "The Bible in the Roman Catholic Church," *Jewish and Christian Traditions,* p. 113.

6. Robert Grant, "Jesus and the Old Testament," *The Authoritative Word: Essays on the Nature of Scripture,* ed. by Donald McKim (Grand Rapids: Eerdmans, 1983), p. 20.

to the Old Testament prophetic view, which sees people directed by God to speak but still uttering fallible words.[7]

2 Timothy 3:16 clearly affirms that Scripture is inspired for the sake of reproof, correction, and instruction in righteousness. (Reference to inerrancy and infallibility of scientific and historical data is in no way implied here.) Inspiration covers the Old Testament, perhaps the Pauline letters, but it would include also the Book of Enoch, which Jude and 2 Peter quote. The definite article in the Greek should be translated as "every" and not "all," which implies a collection of sacred writings, not a canon or official collection.[8] The text seems to imply that God breathes life into the "dead letter" of the Old Testament so that even it may be useful for the religious training of the Christian.[9] Or the text may imply that only those writings of the Old Testament which are inspired may be useful for Christian teaching. Either way the passage hardly says what inspirationists earnestly desire. The passage says nothing about inerrancy or verbal dictation, nor does it speak of a canon of Scripture, nor does it describe the Scriptures as the foundation of Christian theology, and finally it does not even consider the Scriptures as the unique or ultimate criterion of the faith.[10]

The other passage of great significance is 2 Peter 1:20–21. It talks about the origin of prophecy, not the resultant writings. Prophets are trustworthy because they testify to the coming Christ. Whereas 2 Timothy 3:14 attributes the authorship of Scripture to God, 2 Peter 1:21 clearly

---

7. Vawter, *Inspiration,* pp. 8–19; Stephan Davis, *The Debate about the Bible: Inerrancy versus Infallibility* (Philadelphia: Westminster, 1977), pp. 15–140; Clark Pinnock, "Three Views of the Bible in Contemporary Theology," *Biblical Authority,* ed. Jack Rogers (Waco: Word, 1977), pp. 63–87; and Paul Hanson, "The Theological Significance of Contradiction within the Book of the Covenant," *Canon and Authority: Essays in Old Testament Religion and Theology,* ed. George Coats and Burke Long (Philadelphia: Fortress, 1977), p. 131.

8. Smith, "Inspiration," p. 501; and James Barr, *Holy Scripture: Canon, Authority, Criticism* (Philadelphia: Westminster, 1983), p. 25.

9. Hubert Cunliffe-Jones, *The Authority of the Biblical Revelation* (Boston: Pilgrim Press, 1948), pp. 115–116; Richardson, "Biblical Scholarship," p. 313; David Hubbard, "The Current Tensions: Is There a Way Out?" *Biblical Authority,* pp. 172–175; and Paul Achtemeier, *The Inspiration of Scripture: Problems and Proposals,* Biblical Perspectives on Current Issues (Philadelphia: Westminster, 1980), pp. 8–19.

10. J. McKenzie, "Inspiration," p. 390; and Barr, *The Scope and Authority of the Bible* (Philadelphia: Westminster, 1980), pp. 63, 119–120, and *Holy Scripture,* p. 20.

implies the presence of the human factor. The word "impelled" is the same word used to describe a ship blown by the wind (Acts 27:16–17).[11]

In Matthew 5:17–18 Jesus states that the law will not pass away, and inspirationists equate law with Old Testament Scripture, and thereby imply that this statement covers all Scripture. That is an unfortunate equation. Jesus refers to the Mosaic law, a corpus which was seen by Paul and most Christians as a "dead letter," no longer binding. The writer of the Gospel of Matthew wishes to qualify this Pauline understanding by saying that the Mosaic law is no longer binding because Jesus has fulfilled and surpassed the demands of the law. By itself the law would endure forever, and now with the new deepened understanding of the law brought by the Sermon on the Mount, the "new law" will last forever. The expression "jot and tittle" in 5:18 refers in hyperbolic fashion to the stringent demand of particular Mosaic laws; it is not an argument for strict verbal inspiration.[12]

In John 10:35 Jesus declares that the intent or meaning of Scripture is forever true. Such a statement describes the faithfulness of Scripture, but in no way is a concept of inspiration discussed or developed here. The reference to God speaking in the law is too brief to build a theory of inspiration upon it.[13]

In the New Testament only two passages really approach the issue of inspiration: 2 Timothy 3:15 and 2 Peter 1:20–21. However, they are limited in what they say about the phenomenon. Exegetes often bring pre-conceived notions concerning the nature of inspiration to these passages and merely cite the passage to undergird their own particular model.

When viewed in a straightforward fashion the biblical text says very little about inspiration. The Scriptures are more interested in testifying to the gracious actions of God, and, in particular, confessing the importance of Jesus Christ and the resurrection. They offer little or no self-testimony concerning the nature of their divine origin or authority, for that would usurp the authority of God and Jesus Christ.

11. Smith, "Inspiration," p. 502; Robert Alley, *Revolt Against the Faithful: A Biblical Case for Inspiration as Encounter* (New York: Lippincott, 1970), pp. 77–78; and Achtemeier, *Inspiration,* pp. 111–113.

12. Hubbard, "Current Tensions," pp. 172–175; and Achtemeier, *Inspiration,* pp. 111–113.

13. Ibid.

DIFFERENT MODELS OF INSPIRATION

Because of the vague and limited nature of the Bible's own self-testimony about inspiration, a number of different inspiration theories have arisen in the Christian tradition. The ensuing chapters shall seek to evaluate these various models.

Classification of these different models and the theologians who articulate them is arbitrary, just as the larger categories in this work are arbitrarily construed by this author. Other studies offer different classifications which are valid and may be equally helpful in studying the phenomena of inspiration.

Luis Alonso-Schökel classifies inspiration theories along the format of how the inspired speaker is viewed in relationship to God.[14] He divides the theories into three categories: (1) The speaker is the instrument through whom God speaks. (2) The author is the person to whom God dictates the word—herein he includes Roman Catholic and Protestant Scholastic theories of the early modern period. (3) The speaker is the messenger sent by God.

Dewey Beegle offers four classifications, but he does not develop them extensively. These are: (1) intuition, (2) illumination, (3) dictation, and (4) dynamic relationship.[15]

Robert Johnston offers a very helpful typology of conservative or evangelical Protestant views on inspiration. He classifies leading American Protestant theologians into four groups, which may be described in a spectrum of very conservative to less conservative perspectives:[16]

(1) *Detailed Inerrancy.* Advocates include Francis Schaeffer, Harold Lindsell *(Battle for the Bible)* and others who demand that all Christians need to adhere to a total doctrine of Scripture's full inspiration and perfect testimony in the areas of faith, practice, and all matters of science and history. They refuse fellowship to anyone who does not adhere to this position.

(2) *Irenic Inerrancy or Flexible Inerrancy.* Advocates like Clark Pinnock *(Set Forth Your Case: A Defense of Biblical Infallability* and

---

14. Luis Alonso-Schökel, *The Inspired Word: Scripture in the Light of Language and Literature,* trans. Francis Martin (New York: Herder and Herder, 1972), pp. 58–73.

15. Beegle, *Scripture,* pp. 124–125.

16. Robert Johnston, *Evangelicals at an Impasse: Biblical Authority in Practice* (Atlanta: Knox, 1979), pp. 19–34.

Biblical Revelation) and Daniel Fuller suggest that we view the text as infallible (incapable of deception) and inerrant (without error in what it affirms). But we must admit that their views on science and history differ from ours, so what appear to us as errors are not really errors, given their context. Items which are incidental are not part of what Scripture intends to teach; they are non-revelatory matters.

(3) *Complete Infallibility.* Individuals like David Hubbard (president of Fuller Seminary) and Paul Jewett (also of Fuller Seminary) prefer to avoid the word "inerrancy" and use only infallibility. For this will enable theologians to read the Bible in order to address the problems faced by the Church today. The message of the text must be seen beyond the cultural limitations of that era.

(4) *Partial Infallibility.* Writers like Dewey Beegle *(Inspiration of Scripture* and *Scripture, Tradition and Infallibility)* and Stephan Davis *(The Debate About the Bible)* strongly attack the position of inerrancy as rationalistic, obscurantistic, obsessed, and docetic. The Bible has errors in matters of scientific and historical detail, but it is infallible in matters of faith and practice.

Johnston's categories are helpful in studying Protestant Evangelicals, but they are a little too detailed for this work. For our purposes the first two categories will be combined into the position of inerrancy (strict verbal inspiration) and the latter two categories will be combined into the position of infallibility (limited verbal inspiration).

The methodological format of this work will delineate advocates of inspiration into four models. The first group (strict verbal inspiration) declares the very words of the text to be inspired by direct divine communication. The second group (limited verbal inspiration) believes that the words are communicated by God but are historically conditioned or accommodated. The third group believes that inspiration does not really apply to the biblical text as we have it (non-textual inspiration). Some would posit that only the ideas or message is inspired, while others limit the experience of inspiration to the authors who gave us the text and not the text itself. The fourth group creatively posits that inspiration is a charism which affected the community of believers as a whole rather than individual authors (social inspiration).

Chapter Four

STRICT VERBAL INSPIRATION

The stance taken by many conservative Protestants strongly declares that the Bible has authority for the theology and lifestyle of all Christians because it is inspired by God. The actual biblical words are inspired or even dictated by God through the individuality of each biblical author.

Several terms are used characteristically by advocates of this position. The inspiration of not only the thoughts but the very words of the author is called verbal inspiration. In addition, one may speak of the text as being inspired completely and equally in all its parts, and this is called full or plenary inspiration. Advocates also speak of the Bible as being infallible, a truthful and unerring guide in matters of faith and doctrine, and inerrant, which means the Bible does not err in incidental matters of history or science. It is the last term which has engendered the greatest debate among conservative Protestants, and many have balked at accepting the concept of inerrancy by moving to a position of limited verbal inspiration.

The position of total infallibility and inerrancy has been defended zealously during the last two centuries.[1] This view was developed most

---

1. The position may be traced most directly to the work of Francis Turretin (1632–1687), a Calvinistic theologian in the Protestant Age of Orthodoxy, especially his book, *The Doctrine of Scripture,* ed. John Beardslee III (Grand Rapids: Baker, 1981), pp. 7–234. Modern expositions include Louis Gaussen (1790–1863), *"Theopneustia": The Plenary Inspiration of the Holy Scriptures,* trans. David Scott, ed. B.W. Carr (London: Farncombe and Son, 1912), pp. 15–309, whose work was used as a resource by the Princeton theologians; Archibald Alexander, *Evidences of the Authenticity, Inspiration, and Canonical Authority of the Holy Scriptures* (Philadelphia: Presbyterian Board of Publication, 1836), pp. 9–308; Charles Hodge, "What Is Christianity?" *The Biblical Repertory and Princeton*

thoroughly in the nineteenth century in the English-speaking world. Forerunners may be found among some theologians in the age of Protestant Orthodoxy (1600–1750), such as Johann Gerhard (*Loci communes theologica*, 1610–1622), Johann Quenstedt (*Theologica didactica-polemica*, 1657), and Francis Turretin (*Doctrine of Scripture*, 1688). Roman Catholic counterparts may be found in Domingo Bañez (*Scholastic Commentary*, 1584) and Charles Rene Billuart (*Summa Theologica*, 1758).[2] The view has been articulated most clearly by the Reformed theologians of

Review (January 1860), and *Systematic Theology*, 3 vols. (New York: Scribner's, 1899), 1:151–188; Archibald Alexander Hodge and Benjamin Breckenridge Warfield, "Inspiration," *The Presbyterian Review* 7 (April 1881), 225–260; Warfield, *The Inspiration and Authority of the Bible*, ed. Samuel Craig (Philadelphia: Presbyterian and Reformed Publishing Company, 1948; reprint of various works), pp. 71–442; A.A. Hodge, *Outline of Theology* (1897; reprint: Grand Rapids: Eerdmans, 1949), pp. 65–93. Their position has been reaffirmed by recent writers, including: Edward J. Young, *Thy Word Is Truth* (Grand Rapids: Eerdmans, 1957), pp. 13–263; Wallie Criswell, *Why I Preach That the Bible Is Literally True* (Nashville: Broadman, 1969), p. 68 et passim; Rene Pache, *The Inspiration and Authority of Scripture*, trans. Helen Needham (Chicago: Moody, 1969), pp. 45–79, 120–158, et passim, offers a thorough but naive defense of inerrancy; John Warwick Montgomery, ed., *God's Inerrant Word: An International Symposium on the Trustworthiness of Scripture* (Minneapolis: Bethany, 1974), pp. 13–281, contains a number of essays read at Ligonier, Pennsylvania in the fall of 1973 to defend the idea of inerrancy, and, in particular, Pinnock, "Limited Inerrancy: A Critical Appraisal and Constructive Alternative," pp. 143–158, defends traditional inerrancy against views of limited verbal inspiration; John Gerstner, "The Theological Boundaries of Evangelical Faith," *The Evangelicals*, eds. David Wells and John Woodbridge (Nashville: Abingdon, 1975), pp. 21–37; Leon Morris, *I Believe in Revelation* (Grand Rapids: Eerdmans, 1976), pp. 9–159; Harold Lindsell, *The Battle for the Bible* (Grand Rapids: Zondervan, 1976), pp. 17–212, offers a very popular defense of inerrancy in order to arouse people to purge their denominations of preachers and teachers who do not hold to inerrancy; James Montgomery Boice, ed., *The Foundations of Biblical Authority* (Grand Rapids: Zondervan, 1978), pp. 15–156, contains essays devoted to the defense of inerrancy, and particular essays of interest include Gleason Archer, "The Witness of the Bible to Its Own Inerrancy," pp. 85–99, and Robert Sproul, "Sola Scriptura: Crucial to Evangelism," pp. 103–119; Norman Geisler, ed., *Inerrancy* (Grand Rapids: Zondervan, 1979), pp. 2–446, contains essays defending inerrancy, in particular, Paul Feinberg, "The Meaning of Inerrancy," pp. 267–304; Roger Nicole and Ramsey Michaels, eds., *Inerrancy and Common Sense* (Grand Rapids: Baker, 1980), pp. 15–203, contains essays defending inerrancy in more moderate fashion, best represented by Nicole, "The Nature of Inerrancy," pp. 71–95, who defends a view of limited inerrancy; and D.A. Carson and Woodbridge, eds., *Scripture and Truth* (Grand Rapids: Zondervan, 1983), pp. 9–356, contains essays defending traditional inerrancy, in particular essays by Wayne Grudem, "Scripture's Self-Attestation and the Problem of Formulating a Doctrine of Scripture," pp. 19–59, and James Packer, "Infallible Scripture and the Role of Hermeneutics," pp. 325–356.

    2. Alonso-Schökel, *Word*, pp. 58–72.

Princeton Seminary in the nineteenth century: Archibald Alexander (1772–1851), Charles Hodge (1797–1878), Archibald Alexander Hodge (1823–1886), and Benjamin Breckinridge Warfield (1851–1921).[3] They built their understanding upon the theology of Francis Turretin (1632–1687), who developed the Aristotelian or Scholastic view of inerrancy, and Louis Gaussen (1790–1863), a classic reformulation of Turretin.[4] Philosophically they were grounded in the Common Sense Philosophy of Thomas Reid from Scotland, which was popularized in America by John Witherspoon (1723–1794). This philosophy assumed that what was true could be logically demonstrated to all people, since human values were the same everywhere (a naive concept by today's understanding).[5] The combination of Reformed theology and Common Sense Philosophy produced a "biblical positivism" which proceeded to evaluate the Bible inductively, placing priority on reason over faith, and seeking factual evidence to verify the Bible's authenticity. They assumed the human mind to be unaffected by original sin, and therefore capable of producing an unimpeccable theology.[6]

During the course of the nineteenth century the Princetonian position became more conservative in the face of the perceived threat of science. Whereas Hodge could accept a few errors in his infallible Bible ("specks in the fine marble"), Warfield could not, and for him inspired had to mean inerrant. The doctrine of inspiration was the starting point for Warfield's theology, and he felt that other doctrines could not be believed unless the authority of Scripture was undergirded by a firm understanding of inspiration.[7]

Most advocates of strict verbal inspiration admit their indebtedness to Warfield and the Princeton theologians in general. They frequently maintain, however, that views of verbal inspiration and inerrancy were

---

3. Gerstner, "Warfield's Case for Biblical Inerrancy," *God's Inerrant Word*, pp. 115–142; Rogers and McKim, *The Authority and Interpretation of the Bible: An Historical Approach* (New York: Harper and Row, 1979), pp. 3–461, trace this theological tradition from its precedents to its modern successors in very critical and thorough fashion; and Woodbridge and Randall Balmer, "The Princetonians and Biblical Authority: An Assessment of the Ernest Sandeen Proposal," *Scripture and Truth*, pp. 251–279.

4. Turretin, *Scripture*, pp. 7–234; Gaussen, *Inspiration*, pp. 5–365; and Rogers and McKim, *Authority*, who note that Turretin did not quote Calvin in his work, even though he stood in Calvin's tradition, for his view of Scripture departed radically from Calvin's.

5. Rogers and McKim, *Authority*, pp. 235–247.

6. Kelsey, *Scripture*, p. 23; and ibid., pp. 290, 325.

7. Kelsey, *Scripture*, p. 21; and Barr, *Fundamentalism*, p. 263.

affirmed by theologians throughout the history of the Church, and Luther and Calvin are isolated in particular as proponents of this position.[8]

Strict verbal inspirationists have a very high view of the Bible. The words of the Bible are the timeless and eternal communication of God to his people through the mediation of prophets and apostles. The writers of Scripture stood outside the community of faith and were set apart from the normal state of humanity to receive the word of God. Upon reception of this word they were entrusted to teach it to their contemporaries and record it for future generations, that they, too, might have the true word of doctrine. God is the principal author who directs the intellect of the writer infallibly; but the writer does research and uses his own style in conformity with his own talent. Warfield could describe the process of inspiration as sunlight going through stained glass windows—God's revelation is the sunlight and the individual authors are the prism of the glass.[9]

The words of Scripture may be considered absolute truth and used without fear for the articulation of theology and Church practice. The treatment of textual statements in this fashion implies that the text is propositional revelation from God to man. For if God is truthful, and Scripture is revealed by God, then it must be true in all its parts. If God is perfect, and God is revealed in the Bible, the Bible must be perfect. Since not lying entails total and absolute accuracy, and common sense tells us that the accuracy is the same for all people everywhere, then Scripture must be accurate in all its details. This is attested to by Jesus when he said, "Scripture cannot be broken" (Jn 10:35). Further, since God is faithful to his Church, he must have given a faithful source for the theology and practice of the Church. Therefore, Scripture can be trusted to guide every

---

8. Robert Preus, *The Inspiration of Scripture: A Study of the Theology of the Seventeenth Century Lutheran Dogmaticians* (London: Oliver and Boyd, 1957), pp. 76–87; and Gerstner, "The Church's Doctrine of Biblical Inspiration," *Foundations,* pp. 23–58, both do a quick evaluation of the view of various Church Fathers. Luther and Calvin are particularly discussed by Packer, " 'Sola Scriptura' in History and Today," pp. 43–62; Montgomery, "Lessons from Luther on the Inerrancy of Holy Writ," pp. 63–94; Packer, "Calvin's View of Scripture," pp. 95–114, *God's Inerrant Word,* pp. 43–114; Preus, "The View of the Bible Held by the Church: The Early Church Through Luther," pp. 357–382; and Gerstner, "The View of the Bible Held by the Church: Calvin and Westminster Divines," pp. 385–410, *Inerrancy,* pp. 357–410; and Richard Lovelace, "Inerrancy: Some Historical Perspectives," *Common Sense,* pp. 20–26.

9. Warfield, *Inspiration,* p. 156.

action of the Christian.[10] To be sure the text speaks of the men as inspired, but it is logical that if the men are inspired, so are their writings.[11]

It is common for apologists of inerrancy to connect inerrancy of the biblical text to the divinity of Jesus. If Jesus is God, and God does not lie or tell half-truths, then when Jesus quotes the Old Testament, the Old Testament can be seen as inerrant (especially on issues like Mosaic authorship, the unity of Isaiah, Jonah in the whale, etc.). If Christ "accommodated" himself to the limited knowledge of his audience, then we could believe nothing of what he said or did. Therefore, we must accept all of Scripture as inerrant.[12] These logical deductions are the hallmarks of theologians who advocate this position.

Many advocates of this position are familiar with higher criticism and the problems it poses for them. They are particularly sensitive to textual criticism and the presence of variant readings in the biblical text. Therefore, many believe that inerrancy was limited only to the original manuscripts or autographs, and thus variant readings are merely corruptions of later copies. But they hasten to add that no major doctrine is affected. Much energy is expended to explain why, if only the original copies are inerrant, there is any need for the doctrine at all today. Higher criticism may be used (text criticism) to determine what was the original reading and to resolve difficulties in the Bible for the edification of the faithful. But some believe that the whole process by which the Bible has come to us, including textual transmission, has been providentially directed by God.[13] Overall defenders of this viewpoint declare that the Bible

---

10. John Murray, "The Attestation of Scripture," *Infallible Word,* eds. Ned Bernard Stonehouse and Paul Woolley (Philadelphia: Presbyterian Guardian, 1946), pp. 1–52; Beegle, *Scripture,* p. 156; Johnston, *Evangelicals,* p. 38; and Achtemeier, *Inspiration,* p. 50.

11. John Kelman Sutherland Reid, *The Authority of Scripture: A Study of the Reformation Understanding of the Bible* (London: Methuen, 1962), pp. 29–55; Davis, *Debate,* pp. 54, 114–115; and Achtemeier, *Inspiration,* p. 23.

12. Edward John Carnell, *The Case for Orthodox Theology* (Philadelphia: Westminster, 1959), pp. 33–50; Robert Lightner, *The Saviour and the Scriptures: A Case for Scriptural Inerrancy* (Grand Rapids: Baker, 1966), pp. 1–171; Pinnock, "The Inspiration of Scripture and the Authority of Jesus Christ," pp. 201–218; and Sproul, "The Case for Inerrancy: A Methodological Analysis," pp. 242–261, *God's Inerrant Word,* pp. 201–218, 242–261; John Wenham, "Christ's View of Scripture," *Inerrancy,* pp. 3–34; and Gerstner, "A Protestant View of Biblical Authority," *Jewish and Christian Traditions,* pp. 41–63.

13. Warfield, *Inspiration,* p. 156; Young, "The Authority of the Old Testament," pp. 53–87; Stonehouse, "The Authority of the New Testament," pp. 88–136, and John Skilton, "The Transmission of the Scriptures," pp. 137–187, *Infallible Word,* pp. 53–187; and Greg Bahnsen, "The Inerrancy of the Autographa," *Inerrancy,* pp. 151–193.

can be affirmed as the only rational source for theology in a world of modern irrationalism. [14]

In the history of the Church there were some earlier antecedents to this view. Scholastic "instrumental causality" viewed God as the principal efficient cause, like the hand which moves the piece of chalk, which is equivalent to the biblical author, who is the instrumental efficient cause. [15] Later advocates of maximalism, that is, God is the maximal author of Scripture, also moved in similar thought categories. [16] Church historians also notice strong inspiration statements in reformers like Luther and Calvin, although both could utter rather critical pre-modern statements about the text. [17] Dogmatic models of propositional revelation are more typical of seventeenth century orthodox fathers of Lutheranism and Calvinism. [18]

The strength of this position is its clear understanding of the Bible's authority. The Bible is viewed in serious fashion. Christian life, theology, faith, and morals may be clearly and easily propounded by a simple recourse to the biblical text appropriate to the problem. Uniformity is created within a particular community which offers a sense of security and enduring permanence for those who crave such. A firm theological basis will prevent apostasy of faithful believers. A secure base can be constructed for polemics against thought movements in the modern world which are deemed as threats to Christianity. Advocates frequently cite the threat of weakening the faith and eroding the doctrine of historic Christianity, if the principle of inerrancy is surrendered. [19]

Weaknesses abound in the defense of this position, however. Though Hodge and Warfield may have been able defenders of the position in the nineteenth century, many of their followers have been rationalistic and reductionistic in their arguments. The defense of Scripture is under-

---

14. Cornelius Van Til, "Introduction," in Warfield, *Inspiration*, pp. 48–57, who describes Lutheran and Roman Catholic theology as typical forms of irrationalism, for only Calvinist theology can articulate the doctrine of Scripture in authentically rational terms.

15. Vawter, *Inspiration*, pp. 42–57, who maintains that most medieval authors did not view inspiration in this mechanistic fashion; and Achtemeier, *Inspiration*, pp. 25–26.

16. Vawter, *Inspiration*, pp. 58–63, attributes this view to Henry of Ghent, Melchior Cano, his student Domingo Bañez, Pierre d'Ailly, Charles Rene Billuart, and Gregoria di Valencia.

17. Reid, *Authority*, pp. 29–55.

18. Ibid., pp. 72–102.

19. Beegle, *Scripture*, pp. 283–289; Montgomery, "Biblical Inerrancy: What Is at Stake?" *God's Inerrant Word*, pp. 15–42; and Lindsell, *Battle*, pp. 17–212.

taken with rationalistic logic which threatens the "sufficiency of Scripture" more than defending it. Inerrancy is not an expression of respect for Scripture, but it is a religious doctrine which makes arbitrary use of selected portions of the biblical text and subordinates the rest. The "defense" of Scripture becomes more important than Scripture itself or a proper understanding of Scripture. Inerrancy is a concept introduced into the Bible and it becomes the norm to which the Bible is made to conform.[20] Countryman sums it up well:

> . . . they have tacitly abandoned the authority or Scripture in favor of a conservative Protestant theology shaped largely in the nineteenth century. This fundamentalist theology they buttress with strings of quotations to give it a biblical flavor, but it pre-determines their reading of Scripture so completely that one cannot speak of the Bible as having any independent voice in their churches.[21]

This dogmatic position leads to the creation of new theological maxims not taught in the Bible, such as inerrancy, infallibility, verbal and plenary inspiration, so that a hedge must be placed around Scripture in order to protect it. The believers now dictate to God what kind of Bible he must have inspired.[22] Such undue rationalism squeezes the life from the living word of God. Prophecy is reduced to prediction and Jesus' sayings become mere doctrine and social legislation, the antithesis of our Lord's intent. Spokespersons of God are reduced to automatons, puppets on a string.[23] The words are viewed in rationalistic terms as propositions dictated by God which can be treated in objective and systematic fash-

20. James Smart, *The Interpretation of Scripture* (Philadelphia: Westminster, 1961), pp. 183, 193; Pinnock, *Biblical Revelation—The Foundation of Christian Theology* (Chicago: Moody, 1971), pp. 53–106, 158–207, offers a thorough defense of inerrancy and a critique of other positions; Johnston, *Evangelicals*, p. 41; Beegle, *Scripture*, pp. 296–297; Barr, *Scope*, p. 70 and *Holy Scripture*, p. 31; Hubbard, "Current Tensions," pp. 162–167; and Donald Bloesch, "The Primacy of Scripture," *Authoritative Word*, pp. 149–151.

21. Countryman, *Authority*, p. 9.

22. Wolfgang Schweitzer, "Biblical Theology and Ethics Today," trans. Reid, *Biblical Authority for Today: A World Council of Churches Symposium on The Biblical Authority for the Churches' Social and Political Message Today*, eds. Alan Richardson and W. Schweitzer (London: SCM Press, 1951), p. 141; Everett Harrison, "The Phenomena of Scripture," *Revelation and the Bible* (Grand Rapids: Baker, 1958), p. 238; Alley, *Revolt*, pp. 75–97; and Johnston, *Evangelicals*, p. 33.

23. Alley, *Revolt*, pp. 75–97; and Dodd, *Authority*, pp. 21–24.

ion.[24] Advocates seek "the understanding and use of the Bible as an instrument separated from the free grace of God and put into the hands of man."[25]

The Bible is turned into an ideal which is more important than the message it contains. The centrality of Christ or the Gospel is usurped. The Bible is a holy object in which the Christian may experience numinous power. Advocates willingly admit that faith in Christ cannot be the objective starting point for discussion; only the Bible can perform that role, so it gradually becomes the basis for faith in Christ. One cannot be accepted as truly Christian by inerrantists merely by confession of faith in Christ, until one acknowledges a similarly high view of biblical authority.[26]

Advocates must deny the historical development in the greater biblical tradition. Evaluating the biblical material in its social and historical context is discarded in favor of dogmatic and philosophical presuppositions. This prevents the Bible from being read in an effective manner; the text can no longer speak clearly. The variety of literary forms (fiction, poetry, parable, legend, prose) cannot be appreciated nor apprehended, and much meaningful insight is lost. Inerrantists will use critical scholarship as long as they produce conservative results, which means they do not read the text with open minds or hearts. If they truly took the text literally, they would be forced to admit the presence of sources and other conclusions drawn by critical scholars.[27]

Inerrantists cannot deal with scriptural problems such as doublets, mythical elements, and textual inconsistencies, so they ignore them. Insensitivity to differences between historical and mythic language caused

24. Smart, *Scripture*, p. 193; William Abraham, *The Divine Inspiration of Holy Scripture* (Oxford: University Press, 1981), pp. 14–38; and Bloesch, "Primacy," pp. 149–151.

25. Karl Barth, *Church Dogmatics*, Vol. 1: *The Doctrine of the Word of God*, trans. Geoffrey Bromiley and Thomas Torrance (Edinburgh: Clark, 1956), Vol. 1, pt. 2, 523.

26. Regin Prenter, "A Lutheran Contribution," *Symposium*, pp. 98–111; Christopher Evans, "The Inspiration of the Bible," *Recent Studies*, pp. 25–32 = *Theology* 59 (1956): 11–17; Leonard Hodgson, "God and the Bible," *Recent Studies*, pp. 1–24 = *Church Quarterly Review* 159 (1958): 532–546; Smart, *Scripture*, pp. 210–213; Reid, *Authority*, p. 211; Beegle, *The Inspiration of Scripture* (Philadelphia: Westminster, 1963), p. 98; Kelsey, *Scripture*, p. 172; Bernard Ramm, "Is 'Scripture Alone' the Essence of Christianity?" *Biblical Authority*, pp. 112–117; Pinnock, "Three Views," pp. 63–64; and Barr, *Fundamentalism*, p. 312.

27. Barr, *Fundamentalism*, pp. 46, 52, 158; and Ramsey Michaels, "Inerrancy or Verbal Inspiration? An Evangelical Dilemma," *Common Sense*, pp. 58–59.

by the reduction of all statements to mere propositional truths loses the symbolic and artistic power of Scripture. Inconsistencies in the text are either dismissed with weak allegorization or mere avoidance. The rigid position forces their exegetes to prove away any possible error, and they will twist back and forth between literal and non-literal interpretation to obtain harmonization of difficult passages.[28] As James Barr notes:

> The amount of harmonization that is necessary in order to sustain a consistent and detailed fundamentalist understanding of the Bible is very great, and it is probable that very few fundamentalists, apart from scholarly apologists, are aware of the amount involved.[29]

Inerrantists lose their perspective on the important matters, and soon all the ideas in the text receive equal stress, so that a legalistic casuistry develops that elevates trivialities to the core of the faith, and the text is no longer heard. Denominations deeply rooted in this ethos tend to be characterized by a contentious spirit and the potential for strife over the smallest issues. Ecumenical activity is frowned upon as a threat to the true faith, which means the possibility of blurring crucial distinctions on trivial issues.[30]

Strict inspirationalists lose the human side of Scripture with their emphasis upon the divine. This in turn affects Christology, and their loss of the human side of Jesus runs the risk of a modern docetism with its lack of concern for human need, pastoral comfort, and social concerns.[31] The search for objectivity leads to a deification of the Bible, and the deity of Jesus is emphasized as a correlative. Christology is defined to maximize possible shelter for inerrancy, and many appeal to the statements of Jesus concerning the Old Testament to affirm inerrancy. Inerrancy is tied

---

28. Theodore Engelder, *Scripture Cannot Be Broken: Six Objections to Verbal Inspiration Examined in the Light of Scripture* (St. Louis: Concordia, 1944), pp. 3–248, 410–448; and Archer, "Alleged Errors and Discrepancies in the Original Manuscripts of the Bible," *Inerrancy*, pp. 57–82, represent two such attempts. Such attempts are criticized by Barr, *The Bible in the Modern World* (New York: Harper and Row, 1973), pp. 168–175, *Fundamentalism*, pp. 40–46, 268, and *Scope*, pp. 77–78.

29. Barr, *Fundamentalism*, p. 61.

30. W. Schweitzer, "Biblical Theology," pp. 141–142; Hubbard, "Current Tensions," p. 176; and Johnston, *Evangelicals*, p. 33.

31. W. Schweitzer, "Biblical Theology," pp. 147–149; and Pinnock, "Three Views," pp. 61–62.

to the divinity of Jesus like an albatross, and we are warned that both will fall like dominos without each other. All the words of Jesus must be absolutely true in every regard, for if Jesus spoke a culturally accommodated message, his divinity is forfeit. Inerrantists have issued a bold challenge not to their opponents, but to Jesus Christ.[32]

Strict inspirations force their leading exegetes and theologians into a difficult posture. Time and energy must be spent defending the amazing accuracy of the Bible and maintaining that in theory this accuracy is perfect. Every possible "hole in the dike must be plugged."[33] As a result conservative scholars have little time to truly address the issues in the text. When they do treat issues in the Bible, they are unable to solve problems without breaking the barrier of inerrancy established by their denomination. They are forced to become horribly vague or silent. Afraid to address issues of theology and practice in their Church, conservative scholars become a treasure lost to their denomination. The Scriptures are silenced by inerrantists.[34]

Inspiration is confused with authority. Even if the text were dictated by God, the reason for its continued relevance today must depend upon another reason. Inspiration only indicates that the Scriptures were spoken to a people long ago with the highest degree of divine origin. Even the ancient Church felt that not all inspired books belonged in the canon, so they apparently believed that inspiration was not the important reason for the continued use of a writing.[35] Inspiration is significant only after the authority of a text has been established and received by the Christian Church.

Inspiration as articulated by modern evangelicals is not a tenet of historic Christianity. With the present emphasis upon inerrancy and in-

---

32. Barr, *Fundamentalism,* pp. 172, 313; Johnston, *Evangelicals,* p. 38; and Michaels, "Inerrancy," p. 57, points out that they have really confused simple error with falsehood. A culturally conditioned statement does not seek to deceive deliberately. As we translate the Hebrew and Greek, so also we translate culturally and historically conditioned ideas into our own idiom.

33. Bloesch, "Primacy," p. 137.

34. Barr, *Fundamentalism,* pp. 299, 309; Johnston, *Evangelicals,* pp. 17, 33, who is a conservative evangelical, calls upon his colleagues to move beyond talk about the Bible in the abstract to a discussion of the issues raised by the text itself, pp. 1–156; and Bloesch, "Primacy," p. 137.

35. George Anderson, "Canonical and Non-Canonical," *The Cambridge History of the Bible,* Vol. 1: *From the Beginnings to Jerome,* eds. Peter Ackroyd and Evans (Cambridge, England: University Press, 1970), pp. 117–118; Johnston, *Evangelicals,* p. 40; and Hoffman, "Sacred Character," p. 460.

fallibility the belief is stated in categories of modern scientific and empirical thought. The concept of inerrancy advocated is an articulation of the late eighteenth and early nineteenth century, and the classic form arose among the Princeton theologians. Prior to this era, theologians were able to admit the presence of historically conditioned errors in the text. But with the rise of modern science and biblical criticism, the hard position of inerrancy developed. The Bible is said to be truth in the same form as scientific data, yet ironically the fear of such modern science caused the fearful retreat into the concept of strict plenary inspiration.[36]

Conservatives find themselves increasingly at odds with the modern world view, so they retreat into an artificial *Weltanschauung* which attacks modern science and history, produces creation-research societies, and seeks to ban certain textbooks from public schools. This defensive mentality maintains that if one truth falls, everything falls. If one concedes to a weak view of inspiration, then one will fall prey to all the views of liberalism. If a person cannot believe one point, he or she will be led to doubt all. The result of this has often been the disaffection of followers from the movement over minor issues.[37]

Their position is logically incompatible with their own presuppositions. If inerrancy is limited only to original autographs to avoid the issue of textual transmission errors, then no inerrant copy is said to exist today, which is to admit the Church's continued existence with an errant Bible. If so, what is necessary about inerrancy as a belief? Nor has such a high view of Scripture advocated by inerrantists prevented other people from developing strange new sectarian movements within the Protestant Evangelical movement which are unacceptable to the majority of strict inspirationists. If God could have miraculously made an inerrant copy of the Bible, why did he not bother to preserve it (unless he is trying to tell the inerrantists something)? If the original copies alone are inerrant, why do advocates quote 2 Timothy 3:16 to defend inerrancy, since obviously the author of that text had only a copy (which was already in a Greek

36. Arthur Carl Piepkorn, "What Does 'Inerrancy' Mean?" *Concordia Theological Monthly* 36 (1965): 577–593; Smith, "Inspiration," p. 513; Barr, *Fundamentalism*, p. 175; Johnston, *Evangelicals*, pp. 21–22; Abraham, *Holy Scripture*, pp. 14–38, and Achtemeier, *Inspiration*, p. 54.

37. Davis, *Debate*, pp. 15–140; Johnston, *Evangelicals*, p. 33; and John Jefferson Davis, "Genesis, Inerrancy, and the Antiquity of Man," *Common Sense*, pp. 137–159, offers a strange example of the compromise between the biblical world view and modern science.

translation) of the original autograph? Modern inerrantists locate the inspiration in the original autographs in an attempt to exclude the Church from the process of transmitting the text.[38]

Most important of all, the concept of inerrancy does not concur with the biblical material. Inerrantists appeal to 2 Timothy 3:14–17, 2 Peter 1:20–21, Matthew 5:17–18, and John 10:35 to undergird their theory. But these passages say nothing about inerrancy in scientific or historical matters, rather they describe the usefulness of the Old Testament Scriptures for practical theological issues. 2 Timothy 3:16 speaks of their usage for reproof, correction, and instruction in righteousness, and any implications of inerrancy are lacking. 2 Peter 1:20–21 clearly implies the presence of the human factor, a point usually overlooked by inerrantists. Certainly no concrete concept of an existing canon may be found in these passages. Furthermore, Matthew 5:17–18 and John 10:35 do not really refer to the Scriptures as we have them, but to the law of Moses, which stands as something to be fulfilled and surpassed by Jesus. To use these texts to defend inerrancy is self-defeating. In general, the concept of inerrancy has a great deal of difficulty when dealing with the biblical text in its entirety.[39]

In conclusion, the purpose of inerrancy seems questionable. How can inerrancy contribute to a high view of Scripture when it only stresses what Scripture does not do (have errors!) rather than stress what it does.[40] Inerrancy really serves to bolster a theological system for conservative Protestant belief—"Fundamentalism is based on a particular kind of religious tradition, and uses the form, rather than the reality, of biblical authority to provide a shield for this tradition."[41]

---

38. Beegle, *Scripture,* pp. 150–166; and Barr, *Fundamentalism,* pp. 73, 279–284, 297, notes that the flaw in their logic is to assume that the references of Jesus assure historicity and literary authorship—Matthew 12:40 refers to Jonah in the whale, Mark 12:35 refers to Davidic authorship of the Psalms, and Matthew 24:15 refers to Daniel's prophecy.

39. J. McKenzie, "Inspiration," p. 390; Smith, "Inspiration," p. 502; Beegle, *Scripture,* pp. 175–197, discusses a number of biblical texts which simply are impossible for inerrantists to understand without relinquishing their theory; Kelsey, *Scripture,* p. 19; and Barr, *Fundamentalism,* pp. 84–85, and *Holy Scripture,* pp. 20, 25.

40. Davis, *Debate,* pp. 78–82; and Berkeley Mickelsen, "The Bible's Own Approach to Authority," *Biblical Authority,* pp. 63–87.

41. Barr, *Fundamentalism,* p. 11.

Chapter Five

LIMITED VERBAL INSPIRATION

Many people advocate a form of verbal inspiration which is not as strict as the one previously described. Many Protestant Evangelicals have been led to affirm a more flexible definition of inspiration. They frequently speak in terms of the infallibility of Scripture, but not its inerrancy. In this regard, the Roman Catholic positions on verbal inspiration in the nineteenth and twentieth centuries would fit into this category.

Scripture is viewed as inspired and therefore infallible in regard to theology, but it is not inerrant in regard to historical and scientific data, which are historically and culturally conditioned according to the biblical author's context. The authors used the world view of their age, and their scientific, social, and historiographic understandings are different than ours. The language reflects a naive scientific world view, but that does not hinder the religious message.[1] God has assured the correct formulation of the words, but this does not extend to unimportant details. God communicates by accommodation, that is, the Scriptures are expressed through limited human knowledge. Accommodation implies that God uses the limitations of the human being; God is author through the authorship of fallible people. The human author is not a stenographer, but

---

1. Olin Curtis, *The Christian Faith* (London: Eaton and Mains, 1905), p. 77; James Orr, *Revelation and Inspiration* (Grand Rapids: Eerdmans, 1952), p. 177 et passim; Panayotis Bratsiotis, "An Orthodox Contribution," trans. E. Every, *Symposium*, p. 23; Klaas Runia, *Karl Barth's Doctrine of Holy Scripture* (Grand Rapids: Eerdmans, 1962), pp. 81–107; Gerrit Berkouwer, *Holy Scripture* (Grand Rapids: Eerdmans, 1975), pp. 9–366; Beegle, *Inspiration,* pp. 9–193; Davis, *Debate,* pp. 15–140; Richard Coleman, "Biblical Inerrancy: Are We Going Anywhere?" *Theology Today* 33 (1976): 295–303; Paul Rees, "Embattlement or Understanding?" *Biblical Authority,* p. 10; Herman Ridderbos, "The Inspiration and Authority of Holy Scripture," *Studies in Scripture and Its Authority* (Grand Rapids: Eerdmans, 1978), pp. 20–36; Donald Miller, "The Bible," *Authoritative Word,* pp. 107–109; and Bloesch, "Primacy," p. 15.

a living instrument whose personal style and knowledge are used to express divine truth. Scriptures may contain technical inaccuracy, but they are free from willful deception by the "internal witness of the Spirit." Scriptures have essential truth, not absolute truth.[2] The emphasis is not upon the inspiration of individual writers, but more upon the Bible as a whole, for it is the religious message of the whole book which is infallible.

Advocates of this position aver that they stand in the tradition of the great Church Fathers. References from pre-modern theologians are cited to demonstrate their acknowledgement of human limitations in the text despite a high view of authority. Augustine believed that God accommodated himself to the limitations of human comprehension by addressing us as a parent speaks to a child.[3] Luther could affirm the principle of *sola scriptura* but make many critical observations of the text: (1) James contradicts Pauline theology and is inferior, (2) Revelation lacks a Christological emphasis, (3) Jude is merely a copy of 2 Peter, (4) Hebrews was written not by Paul, for it contradicts his theology and contradicts the Gospels by declaring that there could be no second repentance, (5) contradictions exist between the Books of Kings and Chronicles, and (6) discrepancies exist between the Gospel narratives. However, Luther would maintain that such problems did not endanger articles of the faith.[4] Calvin, too, could affirm infallibility without inerrancy. He noted that (1) Moses' understanding of astronomy contradicted modern views, (2) Gospel writers misquoted the Old Testament at times, i.e., Matthew 27:9 misquotes Jeremiah, (3) Peter could not have written 2 Peter, and (4) Revelation was an inferior work in the Bible.[5] Both Luther and Calvin believed that God accommodated himself to the limits of human understanding, the writer's personality, and the historical setting, but this did not imply deception.[6] Defenders of limited verbal inspiration, especially Protestants, can claim a good ancestry in the Church tradition.

---

2. Runia, *Doctrine*, pp. 203–204; Beegle, *Inspiration*, p. 83; Rogers, "The Church Doctrine of Biblical Authority," *Biblical Authority*, pp. 41–46; and Bloesch, "Primacy," p. 139.

3. Greenspahn, "Introduction," *Jewish and Christian Traditions*, p. 163.

4. Kelsey, "Protestant Attitudes," pp. 138–139.

5. Runia, *Doctrine*, pp. 44 et passim; Barr, *Fundamentalism*, pp. 173–174; Rogers and McKim, *Authority*, pp. 109–1114; Kelsey, "Protestant Attitudes," pp. 138–139; and Bloesch, "Primacy," p. 136.

6. Kelsey, "Protestant Attitudes," p. 139.

A number of fine Protestant theologians in the modern era have articulated positions which fall into the spectrum of this general category. Significant theologians include conservative Dutch Calvinists like Herman Bavinck (1854–1921), Abraham Kuyper (1837–1920), Gerrit Cornelius Berkouwer (1903–   ), and Scottish Reformed theologian James Orr (1844–1913). Orr, in particular, was a critic of Benjamin Warfield, and he proposed a more dynamic view of inspiration which concentrated on the entire process by which the text was produced.[7] An increasing number of modern theologians and writers from the Evangelical Protestant movement have begun to endorse this position.[8]

Roman Catholic theologians who affirm verbal inspiration more closely correspond to this position than the more conservative view of inerrancy. Late nineteenth century views of inspiration taught by Marie-Joseph Lagrange and others affirm verbal inspiration with a strong emphasis upon the human element.[9] These theologians were able to for-

---

7. Rogers, "Church Doctrine," pp. 41–46, states that Bavinck and Kuyper clearly taught accommodation; Barr, *Fundamentalism*, pp. 269–270, 294, describes the views of Orr; and Rogers and McKim, *Authority*, pp. 380–393, place Bavinck, Kuyper, and Berkouwer in this category.

8. Curtis, *Faith*, p. 77; Runia, *Doctrine*, pp. 1–219; Beegle, *Scripture*, pp. 7–312; Rees, "Embattlement," p. 10; Ridderbos, "Inspiration," pp. 20–36; Rogers and McKim, *Authority*, pp. xvii–xxiv, 1–471; Coleman, "Inerrancy," pp. 295–303; Michaels, "Inerrancy," pp. 49–70; and Bloesch, "Primacy," pp. 117–153.

9. Marie-Joseph Lagrange, "Une pensee de saint Thomas sur l'inspiration Scripturaire," *Revue de Facultes Catholiques de l'Ouest* (1894) = *Revue biblique* 4 (1895): 563–571, "A propos de l'Encyclique," *Revue biblique* 4 (1895): 48–64, "Inspiration des livres saints," *Revue biblique* 5 (1896): 199–220, "L'Inspiration et les exigences de la critique: Response a la lettre precedente," *Revue biblique* 5 (1896): 496–518, "L'Interpretation de la sainte Ecriture par l'Eglise," *Revue biblique* 9 (1900): 135–142; and *Historical Criticism and the Old Testament*, trans. Edward Myers (London: Catholic Truth Society, 1905), passim. Others included: Levesque, "Questions actuelles d'Ecriture Sainte" and "Essai sur la nature de l'inspiration des livres saintes," *Revue des Facultes Catholiques de l'Ouest* (1894); Herman Schell, *Katholische Dogmatik*, 2 vols. (Paderborn: Schöningh, 1889–189z), passim; Thomas-Marie Pegues, "Une Pensee de Saint Thomas sur l'inspiration scripturaire," *Revue Thomiste* 3 (1895): 95–112; Constantin Chauvin, *L'Inspiration des divines Ecritures* (Paris: Lethielleux, 1896), passim; Jean Bainvel, *De Scriptura Sacra* (Paris: Beauchesne, 1910), passim; Ludovicus Billot, *De Inspiratione Sacrae Theologica Disquisitio*, 2nd ed. (Rome: St. Joseph, 1906), passim; Thomas Calmes, *Qu'est-ce que l'Ecriture Sainte?* (Paris: Bloud, 1899), passim; and Domenico Zanecchia, *Divina Inspiratio Sacrarum Scripturam ad Mentem Sainte Thomae Aquinatis* (Rome: Pustat, 1898), passim. The position articulated by these individuals was later affirmed by Christian Pesch, *De inspiratione Sacrae Scripturae* (Freiburg: Herder, 1906), passim; Benoit Merkelbach, *L'inspiration des divines Ecritures*, 2nd ed. (Liege: n.p., 1913), passim; Jacques Voste, *De divina inspiratione et veritate Sacrae Scripturae* (Rome: n.p., 1932),

mulate their views with the aid of Thomistic philosophy—God was the primary author or principal cause of Scripture, and the human author was the instrumental cause. This enabled them to say that Scripture proceeds equally from God and from human authors. God used human authors in their freedom, so that the message came to us without errors, but it is in the conditioned language of that era.[10]

Modern Roman Catholics often affirm verbal inspiration, but use less of the old Thomistic categories and methods employed by Lagrange and his followers. The emphasis is placed upon affirming divine authorship without diminishing the freedom of the human authors.[11] Inspiration assures that human powers of research and compilation provide an edifying document for the Church. Particular errors in the text do not interfere with this purpose, especially if those "errors" are a cultural reflection of the era in which the document was created. Inerrancy is generally rejected as a viable option in the discussion of inspiration.[12] The Catholic opinion is best reflected by John Scullion:

> But because of its very negative connotations and associations, of its defensive mentality, of the timorous attitude that it displays, I think that it would be better to drop the word "inerrancy" from the theological vocabulary. The word is not characteristic of ecclesiastical documents.[13]

passim; Augustin Bea, *De Scripturae Sacrae inspiratione,* 2nd ed. (Rome: n.p., 1935), passim; and Hildebrand Höpfl and Louis Leloir, *Introductio generalis in Sacram Scripturam,* 6th ed. (Naples: n.p., 1958), passim. The work of these authors is described excellently by Burtchaell, *Catholic Theories,* pp. 121–163.

10. Jean Pirot, "Inspiration," *Guide to the Bible: An Introduction to the Study of Holy Scripture,* 2 vols., ed. Andre Robert and Alphonse Tricot, trans. Edward Arbez and Martin McGuire (Rome: Desclee, 1951), 1:15; Smith, "Inspiration," p. 508; Burtchaell, *Catholic Theories,* pp. 121–163; Vawter, *Inspiration,* pp. 98–99.

11. Wilfrid Harrington, *Record of Revelation: The Bible* (Chicago: Priory, 1965), pp. 27, 43; Scullion, *Theology,* pp. 67–89; Johann Michl, "Scripture," *Encyclopedia of Biblical Theology,* ed. Johannes Bauer (New York: Crossroad, 1981), p. 821; and Dulles, "Catholic Perspective," pp. 23–27.

12. Harrington, *Record,* p. 47; Norbert Lohfink, "The Truth of the Bible and Historicity," *Modern Biblical Studies,* ed. Dennis McCarthy and William Callen (Milwaukee: Bruce, 1967), pp. 43–48; Oswald Loretz, *The Truth of the Bible,* trans. David Bourke (New York: Herder, 1968), p. viii, who expressly seeks to refute the concept of inerrancy; Smith, "Inspiration," pp. 513–514; Scullion, *Theology,* pp. 67–89; and Dulles, "Catholic Perspective," p. 27.

13. Scullion, *Theology,* p. 63.

Further, modern Roman Catholic theologians frequently outline the limitations which must be placed on the concept of verbal inspiration. In this regard, they are more bold than their Protestant counterparts, who must tread lightly in their tradition where the principle of *sola scriptura* has made members sensitive about describing the Bible's "limitations." Roman Catholic scholars often observe the following hermeneutical principles: (1) We must consider the intellectual stage of development; the biblical author's views on science and history differ from ours. (2) We must consider literary forms; whether the text is prose or poetry determines how literally we interpret it. We must be sensitive to their frequent use of symbolic language, myth, legend, and epic forms in communicating truth. (3) We must perceive the original intent of the author when he or she first spoke those words in the social and historical context. This means being sensitive to idiomatic usage in language. This also means that we do not try to get more meaning out of one particular text than the original author may have intended. (4) We must understand the meaning of a particular biblical text in the context of the Scriptures as a whole. With these caveats in mind the Roman Catholic exegete affirms verbal inspiration and seeks to interpret the text in a literal-historical fashion. The truthfulness or infallibility of the Bible refers to its faithfulness in conveying religious insight, not an intellectual certitude in modern scientific-empirical categories.[14]

The strengths of this position are several. The advocates avoid many pitfalls and problems of the former position, and it becomes easier for them to defend a position of scriptural inspiration with intellectual respectability. They are freed from the mission of defending a rigid view of inspiration, a task which diverts their scholarship and intellectual activity from more meaningful issues in biblical studies. A very effective way of avoiding the dogmatic debate is to refrain from using both concepts of inerrancy and infallibility and use terms like truthfulness and trustworthiness.[15]

Second, the position reflects biblical data in more valid fashion. Advocates are able to draw upon many biblical texts to defend their position,

---

14. Harrington, *Record*, pp. 46–53; J. McKenzie, "Inspiration," pp. 392–393; Smith, "Inspiration," pp. 513–514; Scullion, *Theology*, pp. 67–89; Michl, "Scripture," p. 822.

15. Davis, *Debate*, pp. 15–140; and Johnston, *Evangelicals*, pp. 36–37.

and they are more sensitive to the context from which biblical material is taken. Affirming verbal inspiration is not incompatible with modern critical scholarship, if verbal inspiration is understood properly to exclude rigid inerrancy.[16]

Third, the view conforms more closely to that of the Church Fathers in the pre-modern period. For they held to a high view of inspiration but could be quite critical of individual passages. Inerrancy is a creation of the modern Christian world.[17] Furthermore, "it is historically irresponsible to claim that for two thousand years Christians have believed that the authority of the Bible entails a modern concept of inerrancy in scientific and historical details."[18]

Fourth, they move away from static rationalistic approaches to the biblical text which reduce the Bible to propositional revelation.[19] With this view the exegete can more critically evaluate the text and accept it as authoritative at the same time. If necessary, the exegete may challenge a particular text or its interpretation with the aid of another text or insight gleaned from Scripture.[20] This will prevent theological "dead-ends" from arising within a particular tradition.

However, there are problems which arise with this position. The advocates of the strict view of inspiration can accuse this position of intellectual inconsistency. If all knowledge is true and unified, how can something be true and not true at the same time? How can it be binding and not binding upon the believer? This position is internally inconsistent according to conservative critics. How can something be infallible but still have potential for error?[21] Liberal evangelicals wish for the advantages of both positions—the binding authority of a strict inspiration view for doing theology and the freedom of a more flexible view in order to treat difficult textual problems. It appears to be only a "watered-down"

---

16. Barr, *Fundamentalism*, p. 287; and Johnston, *Evangelicals*, p. 36.

17. Gabriel Herbert, *The Authority of the Old Testament* (London: Faber and Faber, 1947), p. 98; Beegle, *Inspiration*, pp. 119–120; Rees, "Embattlement," p. 12; and Rogers, "Church Doctrine," p. 21.

18. Rogers, "Church Doctrine," p. 44.

19. Ibid., pp. 17–46, maintains that this Scholastic Aristotelian approach was introduced to the modern period and to the Princeton theologians in particular by the Reformed theologian Francis Turretin in his work, *Institutio theologicae elencticae* (1623–1687). The Church has more commonly affirmed a Platonic view which implies accommodation.

20. Davis, *Debate*, p. 16.

21. Montgomery, "What Is at Stake," p. 26.

version of inerrancy which does not have the courage to debate the issues and affirm the total doctrine of inerrancy.[22]

How does one distinguish between matters of faith which are infallible and details which may be inaccurate? Are they not often closely connected in the mind of the biblical author? How do we separate one without losing the other? What is then meant by "trivial details"—battle statistics or the way in which biblical authors viewed their world surroundings? Who will decide what is trivial? A great many subjective decisions need to be made by the exegete.[23]

This position seems to introduce a new authoritative principle for determining the message of Scripture—"good common sense"—or what appears to be so in the mind of the exegete. In reality, modern historical and scientific categories became determinative hermeneutical guidelines rather than an emphasis upon the internal witness of the Spirit. Conservatives offer this criticism in particular. "It is a suicidal position that rests the case for Christianity on the shifting sands of scientific and historical research."[24]

Many advocates of this position find themselves tied down in a new debate—the critique of the more rigid position of inerrancy. Scholars find themselves debating the hermeneutical viewpoints of colleagues more conservative than themselves, often in their own denomination. They are compelled to search for contradictions in details in order to disprove inerrancy, but they dare not find major problems or contradictions in matters of faith or doctrine, lest they disprove infallibility. The result is a contorted scholarly quest which may also prevent an objective study of the Bible and keep the text from proclaiming a relevant message to modern problems.[25]

Finally, is the problem really solved by merely watering down the earlier view of inspiration? The more flexible view still sees inspiration as communication of words and ideas by God. The particular words may err, since they are historically accommodated to human understanding, but the ideas are infallible. Why continue to use the concept of divine communication, for this seems to be something other than communication? This merely weakens the concept of inspiration, and if it is the model

22. Johnston, *Evangelicals,* p. 37.
23. Ibid., pp. 25–28; and Nicole, "Nature," p. 72.
24. Bloesch, "Primacy," p. 137.
25. Johnston, *Evangelicals,* pp. 25–28.

being used to assert the authority of the Bible, then the positive dynamic thrust to affirm biblical authority is blunted.[26] The definition of inspiration as communications needs to be changed, for then the somewhat artificial concept of accommodation would no longer be necessary.

The alternative is to seek a model of inspiration which is not connected to the written biblical text. Such theories of inspiration were proposed by liberal Protestant theologians in the last two centuries, who suggested that inspiration applied only to the ideas in the text or to the individuals who first proclaimed the word of God.

---

26. Ibid., p. 37.

Chapter Six

NON-TEXTUAL INSPIRATION

Theologians in the nineteenth and twentieth centuries, many of who were part of a liberal theological tradition, associated inspiration with something other than the words of the biblical text. In this way they sought to avoid the problems which arose with a theory of verbal inspiration. Some theologians believed that only the ideas expressed in Scripture were inspired, while others limited inspiration as an experience of the individuals who first spoke the word of God. The latter theory left inspiration separated completely from the biblical text. Advocates of both positions no longer needed to concern themselves with difficulties which arose in the text, nor did they worry about such terms as inerrancy or infallibility.

INSPIRATION OF IDEAS

The first of these two positions declares that only the ideas or content is inspired, while the words are totally the product of humans conditioned by their cultural and historical circumstances. The formal part of Scripture, the content, is inspired, while the material part of Scripture, the verbal expressions of the author, is not. Different ways of describing this phenomenon are found among various writers—inspiration is ascribed to the essential content, the ideas, matters of faith and morals, doctrinal matters, important themes, quasi-technical concepts, or the essential message. The word of God though mixed with erring words of men and women can speak authoritatively, because it speaks from the depth of authentic human experience. This word still has the ability to effect change in people.

A number of both Protestant and Roman Catholic theologians may

be associated with this view. Typical Protestant advocates include Johann
Semler (eighteenth century), William Robertson Smith (nineteenth cen-
tury), Harold DeWolf and Hans Werner Bartsch (twentieth century).[1]
Many Roman Catholic minimalists and advocates of "content inspira-
tion" (*realinspiration* or the *res et sententiae* position) of the nineteenth
century would belong in this category. Individual theologians include
Lessius, Marcantonio de Dominis, Henricus Holden, and P. Chrismann
in the pre-modern period, and John Henry Newman, Johannes Perrone,
Johann Scholz, Franciscus Patritius, Joseph Kleutgen, August Rohling,
Johannes Franzelin, Francois Lenormant, Thomas Lamy, Hugo Hurter,
Franz Hettinger, Ubaldo Ubaldi, Augusto Berta, Salvatore di Bartolo,
Franciscus Schmid, Peter Dausch, Paul Schanz, and Christian Pesch in
the last two centuries.[2] The two names most often associated with this
view are John Henry Newman and Cardinal Johannes Franzelin.

---

1. William Neil, "The Criticism and Theological Use of the Bible, 1700–1950,"
Cambridge History, 3:287–288; Kraus, *Geschichte*, p. 108; Reid, *Authority*, p. 154; Kelsey, *Scripture*, pp. 24–29; and Achtemeier, *Inspiration*, p. 24, 137–141. A good example
of theology constructed on this model is Harold DeWolf, *A Theology of the Living Church*
(New York: Harper and Row, 1953), pp. 68–86 et passim.

2. F.J. Crehan, "The Bible in the Roman Catholic Church from Trent to the Present
Day," *Cambridge History*, 3:217–222, 229; J. McKenzie, "Inspiration," p. 391; Smith,
"Inspiration," pp. 510–511; Burtchaell, *Catholic Theories*, pp. 58–120, offers the best
review of this material; and Vawter, *Inspiration*, pp. 67–70. Works by significant individ-
uals who affirm this position include: Marcantonio de Dominis, *De Republica Ecclesiastica*
(Hanover, Hulsius, 1622), passim; Henricus Holden, *Diviniae Fidei Analysis* (Paris: So-
cius, 1652), passim; P. Chrismann, *Regula fidei catholicae* (Kempten: n.p., 1792), passim;
John Henry Newman, *Tracts for the Times: Lectures on the Scripture, Proofs of the Doctrines of the Church* (London: Rivington, 1838), passim, *An Essay on the Development of
Christian Doctrine*, 2nd ed. (London: Longmans, 1903), passim, "On the Inspiration of
Scripture," *The Nineteenth Century* 15 (1884): 185–197, and *Inspiration*, pp. 101–153;
Johannes Perrone, *Praelectiones Theologicae* (Taurini: Marietti, 1835–1842), passim; Jo-
hann Martin Augustin Scholz, *Einleitung in den heiligen Schriften* (Cologne: Boisseree,
1845), passim; Franciscus Patritius, *Commentationes* (Rome: Artium, 1851), passim; Jo-
seph Kleutgen, *Die Theologie der Vorzeit*, 2nd ed. (Münster: Theissing, 1867), passim;
August Rohling, "Die Inspiration der Bibel und ihre Bedeutung für freie Forschung,"
Natur und Offenbarung 18 (1872): 97–108; Johannes Baptista Franzelin, *Tractatus de Divina Traditione et Scriptura*, 2nd ed. (Rome: SPF, 1875), passim; Hugo Adalbert Hurter,
Theologiae Dogmaticae Compendium, Vol. 1: *Theologia Generalis* (Innsbruck: Wagner,
1876), passim; Thomas Joseph Lamy, *Introduction in Sacram Scripturam*, 3rd ed. (Mech-
liniae: Dessain, 1877), passim; Ubaldo Ubaldi, *Introductio in Sacram Scripturam* (Rome:
SPF, 1878), passim; Franz Hettinger, *Lehrbuch der Fundamental-Theologie oder Apolo-
getic* (Freiburg: Herder, 1879), passim; Francois Lenormant, *Les origines de l'histoire
d'apres la Bible et les traditiones des peuples orientaux* (Paris: Maisonneuve et Cie, 1880–

Newman believed that Scripture had authority in matters of faith and morals, but the rest of the text, the *obiter dicta,* was not binding and could contain human error, for inspiration described theological content, not details. He believed that the words of Scripture were defective because of the medium of human language. This human finitude could produce *obiter dicta,* statements not binding on our faith. Newman used this concept to emphasize the central message in Scripture over against trivialities and to deal with passages which were not true in their apparent surface meaning. The human and the divine were related in Scripture like the divine and human reality in the sacraments. Ultimately the Church taught truth and the Scripture merely verified its teaching.[3] Newman's views appear to have been condemned by Leo XIII in *Providentissimus Deus* in 1893, but many believe he was vindicated by ideas in the Constitution on Divine Revelation at Vatican II.[4]

The views of Cardinal Franzelin and others predominated in the Roman Catholic Church and undergirded the discussions of Vatican I (1870) on Scripture. According to Franzelin the authors of Scripture received ideas, thoughts, and judgment (formal element) by means of supernatural illumination, but the words and phrases (material element) were the creation of the authors. Franzelin's views would simply fade in popularity with the rise of Lagrange's theories in the 1890's.[5]

1884), passim; Franciscus Schmid, *Die Inspirationis Bibliorum Vi et Ratione* (Brixinae: Weger, 1885), passim; Augusto Berta, *La Bibblia e le Scienza Profane* (Torino: Speirani, 1887), passim; Salvatore di Bartolo, *I Criteri Theologici* (Torino: Giuseppe, 1888), passim, and *Les critieres theologiques* (Paris: Berche and Tralin, 1889), passim; Peter Dausch, *Die Schriftinspiration: Eine biblischgeschichtliche Studie* (Freiburg: Herder, 1891), passim; Paul Schanz, "Zur Lehre der Inspiration," *Theologische Quartelschrift* 77 (1895): 188–204, and *A Christian Apology,* Vol. 2, trans. Michael Glancy and Victor Schobel (Dublin: Gill, 1892), passim; and Christian Pesch, *Praelectiones Dogmaticae,* Vol. 1 (Frieburg: Herder, 1891), passim, and *De Inspiratione Sacrae Scripturae* (Freiburg: Herder, 1906), passim, all of whom are excellently reviewed by Burtchaell, *Catholic Theories,* pp. 58–120.

3. Newman, *Inspiration,* pp. 5, 15, 56, 69, 133, 142; and Burtchaell, *Catholic Theories,* pp. 65–79.

4. Crehan, "Bible," pp. 227–230; Reid, *Authority,* pp. 18–24; Scullion, *Theology,* p. 35; Vawter, *Inspiration,* p. 136; but Murray, ed., *Inspiration* by Newman, pp. 3–6, 15, 26, 68, 92, 102–153, maintains that Newman's position is more complex than the *obiter dicta* generalization implies, for Newman used it as a polemical concept against mechanistic views of inspiration, and he believed that any concept of inspiration or infallibility should be subordinate to the authority of the Church.

5. Pirot, "Inspiration," p. 14; Paul Synave and Benoit, *Prophecy and Inspiration,* trans. Avery Dulles and Thomas Sheridan (Paris: Desclee, 1961), p. 91; J. McKenzie,

The primary strength of this position is the avoidance of controversy associated with word inspiration, whether it be ideas of plenary and verbal inspiration or accommodation. It avoids the bad effects of strict inspiration views—dogmatism, legalism, new doctrinal formulations, violent controversies within Church groups, and modern world views may be accepted. The model emphasizes theological insight and does not worry about details, for the divine origin of the content is affirmed. This emphasizes the "primacy of religion in the Bible." Finally, biblical research may advance, because the diversity of literary styles associated with different authors is recognized.[6]

The chief weakness is an inability to distinguish clearly between unimportant details and the core message. What is an "idea" and what is merely a way of expressing it? That division is left to the subjective opinion of each interpreter. The model is still founded upon an inspiration model, but now God is seen as placing only ideas into the minds of human authors.

God and the human author are juxtaposed causes producing different parts of the Scripture. Can such distinction be made between the words of the authors and the ideas they seek to express?[7] Linguists and psychologists deny this emphatically. The human mind is divided—God is seen to control the inner mind without affecting the external mind, the aspect of speech and communication. One cannot separate words and ideas, especially when certain expressions carry an emotive level which has a particular nuance of meaning.[8]

The position identifies the important aspect of religion with ideas. This overidentifies religion and religious experience with the intellectual aspect. Religion is equated with doctrine. The emotive aspect loses its authoritative undergirding. This would strip value from literature like the Psalms, whose purpose is to provide an emotional religious expression. How can inspiration cause thought, but not emotion, and does not emo-

---

"Inspiration," p. 391; Smith, "Inspiration," pp. 505–508; and Burtchaell, *Catholic Theories*, p. 99.

6. Synave and Benoit, *Prophecy*, p. 91; and J. McKenzie, "Inspiration," p. 391.

7. Scullion, *Theology*, p. 27; and Beegle, *Inspiration*, pp. 78–79.

8. Synave and Benoit, *Prophecy*, p. 91; Beegle, *Inspiration*, pp. 78–79; Smith, "Inspiration," p. 511; Pache, *Inspiration*, pp. 58–62, 71–79; Scullion, *Theology*, p. 27; and Michaels, "Inerrancy," p. 56.

tion produce a particular mode of expression? Inspiration is no longer extended to the totality of the text.[9]

Finally, this model has not really removed the possibility of "error" threatening theological discourse. If the ideas alone are inspired, how can we be sure that an inspired idea may be erroneously presented by the purely human and fallible words?[10] What we have is only a watered-down version of earlier inspiration models, which now works without either inerrancy or infallibility and has de-emphasized the divine so as to make the position nebulous enough for the comfort of theologians.

Inspiration of Individuals

Another way of understanding inspiration avoids this bifurcation of the biblical text and the tendency to make the biblical authors schizophrenic. It avoids attributing inspiration to the text. Inspiration is associated only with the initial experiences of the biblical spokespersons but not the writings. Since the writings often were produced by different individuals than the authors, true prophetic and apostolic inspiration cannot be attributed to those who directly created our Bible. Inspiration was directly experienced by the first spokespersons and only indirectly experienced by the text. Inspiration is an attribute of people, not objects.

This inspiration may refer to a divine-human encounter, or it may refer merely to the religious genius of an extremely sensitive individual.[11] The Bible has authority because it contains the record of religious genius, the communion of people with the divine force either inside or outside themselves. Their insight still communicates to us, and this is the source of the Scripture's authority. Inspiration of the text is secondary or derived from the religious genius of the individuals. This religious genius has authority today when it confronts us with its ability to create religious community, relive the experiences of those individuals, persuade us to respond, and present Christ to us in the form of his spiritual genius. Levels of inspiration exist according to the degree of divine truth expressed in an individual text.[12]

9. Synave and Benoit, *Prophecy*, p. 128; and J. McKenzie, "Inspiration," p. 791.

10. Synave and Benoit, *Prophecy*, pp. 119–120.

11. Alley, *Revolt*, pp. 97–102.

12. Dodd, *Authority*, pp. 27–28, 130, 264–270; Orr, *Revelation*, p. 162; Vawter, *Inspiration*, pp. 89–90; and Achtemeier, *Inspiration*, pp. 41–47.

Advocates of this viewpoint have been usually Protestant liberals of the past two centuries. Under the impulse of Romanticism Johann Gottfried Herder first gave expression to this view. He was followed by later German idealists, the confessional Erlangen school of theology, J.J. Griesbach, J.D. Griesbach, J.E. von Hoffman (who spoke of a *gemeingeist*), and Martin Kähler. In the English-speaking world the classic expression was given by William Sanday in the 1893 *Bampton Lectures*, later by Harry Emerson Fosdick in America (who saw the Bible as the record of spiritual evolution), and Charles Dodd, the best modern advocate of the position.[13] Among Roman Catholic theologians Jacques Bonfrere may be highlighted, for he believed that individual prophets were inspired with "antecedent inspiration," but the books have only a later "concomitant inspiration," the mere preservation from error.[14]

Moderation between the conservative extreme of viewing the Bible as a book of dogma and the liberal extreme of seeing it only as an ancient document remains the chief strength of this position.[15] Further, the scholar may now be thoroughly critical of the text—both words and ideas. The scholar may use the critical tools to discern a new and deeper message for the Church on relevant issues.

Advocates appreciate more deeply the mystical experience; they are more aware of anthropological and sociological understandings of prophetic figures. They often are more aware of religious and mystical phenomena experienced in other religious traditions. Central aspects of the faith are emphasized, and religious and spiritual insights are highlighted.

However, this approach loses the canon as a norm or authority and replaces it with the very subjective notion of religious genius. How can the religious experiences of people long dead be authoritative today? If all we have is a text, and the text is not authoritative, we have nothing.

---

13. Smart, *Scripture,* pp. 216–219; Richardson, "Biblical Scholarship," p. 313; Reid, *Authority,* pp. 164–176; Bryant, *Authority,* p. 21; and Abraham, *Holy Scripture,* pp. 39–57, gives a good discussion of Sanday whom he critiques as having an underdeveloped theory. Good expressions of this position are given by William Sanday, *Inspiration: Eight Lectures on the Early History and Origin of the Doctrine of Biblical Inspiration,* 3rd ed., Bampton Lectures for 1893 (London: Longmans, Green, and Company, 1896), pp. 391–431; and Harry Emerson Fosdick, *A Guide to Understanding the Bible* (New York: Harper and Brothers, 1938), pp. 1–298, and *The Modern Use of the Bible* (New York: Macmillan, 1925), pp. 1–294.

14. Jacques Bonfrere, *In Totam Scripturam Sacram Praeloquia* (1625), as quoted in Burtchaell, *Catholic Theories,* p. 47.

15. Dodd, *Authority,* p. 270.

Advocates speak of the text inspiring people today, but they do not explain how this process is to occur.

Why cannot religious literature from any religious tradition be accepted as authoritative if it shows religious genius? The literature of India, such as the Upanishads and the teachings of Buddha, is universally recognized as being composed of sophisticated and deeply religious documents. Why not receive them as authoritative in the doing of theology? If inspiration is so defined, how do we exclude the religious genius and great literature of other religious traditions? This position requires some additional norm to distinguish which religious literature may be authoritative.

The idea of a religious genius is not a biblical category. The Bible recognizes those who have a divine revelation as being inspired, but it does not include the merely human perspective of someone devoutly religious, insightful, and sensitive. Often the person who has had a revelation is placed in opposition to the wise, religious, and intelligent people of this world. It appears that the category of inspiration may overlap the image of a religious genius at times, but often it stands in distinction.[16]

Since this view usually affirms the ongoing religious and spiritual development of people, why should this religious development have reached its pinnacle and stopped two thousand years ago? We should look to our present world for examples of religious genius, not the biblical authors of millennia past. We should look to the present reality of the living Christ, not the tired sayings of the ancient Church. If this argument is pursued, it becomes evident that not only is the Bible lost as a theological authority, but one is obliged to discard it.

The liberal view of inspiration is self-destructive, for it limits the concept of inspiration until it refers only to subjective religious feelings. What are the categories to distinguish mere feeling from true genius? What about so many new movements or faiths that have sprung up within our land—are they not products of religious genius? What norm shall be used to disinguish between the various manifestations of religious genius? The Bible contains writings of apostles and prophets, not geniuses. The

---

16. Richardson, "Biblical Scholarship," pp. 314–316; and Smart, *Scripture*, p. 219.

former have divine commission, the latter have great human insight, and the former alone are able to do theology.[17]

Individuals are part of a community. It is myopic to eulogize religious experience and forget that genius must be provided with psychological support groups, the community of faith, or it dies. Advocates of this position articulated their views in an age when individualism was emphasized (nineteenth century), and there was less knowledge about the sociological relationship between groups and individuals; hence the inspired speaker's relationship to the community of faith was not considered.

The problem which plagues all inspiration theories and this one especially is the narrow view of prophecy which is presumed. The prophet is one seen to be possessed by the spirit of God, much akin to the Greek concept of the mantic seized by the *daimon,* and this seizure is somehow the locus of religious genius or the source of the message. Such a model might apply to Ezekiel, but it does not describe the activity of Jeremiah and countless other individuals in the biblical tradition, especially Jesus. The diversity of prophets, apostles, and other spokespersons found within the canon defies the narrow romantic mold of religious genius.[18]

Finally, such a position is often used by scholars who seek not to discern what lies in the text, but they produce an ideal (such as the historical Jesus) which conforms to their vision of a religious genius. Scholars often produce an image of a particular personage or a theological perception which reflects more the era in which they live rather than the biblical era. Advocates of this theory often produce a romantic image of the inspired individual which reflects the popular intellectual imagery of the nineteenth century and the liberal idealistic ethos of that age. Their presuppositions produce their own vision.[19]

This theory really moves too far away from the biblical text and becomes a separate ideological theory apart from any discussion of biblical authority. It overlooks especially the concept of biblical community, the source of the inspired individual. In this regard, more recent theories have sought to redress the indifference paid to the community of faith.

---

17. Soren Kierkegaard, "Of the Difference between a Genius and an Apostle," (1847), *The Present Age* (Oxford: University Press, 1940), pp. 137–163; and Cunliffe-Jones, *Authority,* p. 78.

18. Achtemeier, *Inspiration,* pp. 29–32, 48–50, 75, 99–104.

19. W. Schweitzer, "Biblical Theology," p. 143.

Chapter Seven

SOCIAL INSPIRATION

Greater sensitivity to the biblical text and its complex process of development has led to a modern theory of inspiration. Biblical scholars perceive that the text is often produced by more than one individual. The word in oral form is proclaimed by prophets, poets, preachers, bards, and epic historians, while redactors and scribes edit the written word with the addition of their theological insights and commentary. To perceive that Scripture is the product of a process rather than a single setting has led James Barr to say,

> If there is inspiration at all, then it must extend over the entire process of production that has led to the final text. Inspiration therefore must attach not to a small number of exceptional persons . . . it must extend over a larger number of anonymous persons . . . it must be considered to belong more to the community as a whole.[1]

---

1. Barr, *Holy Scripture,* p. 27, and he also expresses the same opinion in *Fundamentalism,* pp. 288–289, and *Scope,* pp. 124–125. Similar views have been expressed by other scholars, especially Roman Catholics: Roderick McKenzie, "Some Problems in the Field of Inspiration," *Catholic Biblical Quarterly* 20 (1958):1–8; Synave and Benoit, *Prophecy,* pp. 123–127, Benoit, "The Analogies of Inspiration," *Aspects of Biblical Inspiration,* trans. Jerome Murphy-O'Connor and S.K. Ashe (Chicago: Priory, 1965), pp. 24–26, and "Inspiration," p. 17, where he speaks of "collective inspiration"; Harrington, *Record,* pp. 39, 45, who speaks of "scriptural inspiration"; Dennis McCarthy, "Personality, Society, and Inspiration," *Theological Studies* 24 (1963): 553–576 = *Modern Biblical Studies,* pp. 18–30; Smith, "Inspiration," p. 510, speaks of "material contributors" and "design contributors," and inspiration lies more with the latter group; William Heidt, *Inspiration, Canonicity, Texts, Versions, Hermeneutics—A General Introduction to Sacred Scripture,* Old Testament Reading Guide, Vol. 31 (Collegeville: Liturgical Press, 1970), p. 13; and Alonso-Schökel, *Word,* pp. 217–224, who speaks of "successive inspiration."

Many other exegetes and theologians are coming to the same conclusion as Barr.

Thus a new understanding of inspiration perceives it to be a charism which was visited upon the entire community rather than upon specific individuals. Individuals in the process who produced the Scriptures were frequently anonymous, for they articulated the faith of the believing community and they expressed themselves as representatives of that corporate entity. The writings therefore are a product of the community, and inspiration resided in that community primarily, whether it was the Yahwistic circles in Israel or the ancient Christian Church. This theory is commonly called the social inspiration theory, and its best advocates are chiefly Roman Catholic in persuasion.[2]

Theologians and exegetes who espouse this view often claim to follow the lead of Pierre Benoit and Karl Rahner in the development of their views. Several scholars synthesize Rahner's social theory of inspiration with Benoit's discussion of how inspiration affects the individual to produce their concept of social inspiration.[3] This inspiration is seen as a charism of the community as a whole and covers the entire process of producing Scripture.

Pierre Benoit was a Scripture scholar who devoted a great amount of study to the phenomenon of the inspiration.[4] His clarifications have been useful for contemporary discussion. (1) He defined inspiration in its broadest sense as an "impulse to do something (act, speak, or write)"

2. Good evaluations of the position are given by John Topel, "Rahner and McKenzie on the Social Theory of Inspiration," *Scripture* 16 (1964): 33–44; and Vawter, *Inspiration*, pp. 104–113.

3. Topel, "Social Theory," pp. 33–44; and Harrington, *Record*, pp. 119–132.

4. Benoit (with Synave), *Prophecy*, pp. 15–168; "La Septante est-elle inspiree?" *Vom Wort des Lebens* (Münster: Westf., 1951), pp. 41–49 = *Exegese et Theologie*, 3 vols. (Paris: Cerf, 1961–1968), 1:3–12; "Inspiration," *A Guide to the Bible*, 1:9–64 = *Initiation Biblique*, eds. Andre Robert and Andre Tricot (Tournai: n.p., 1954), pp. 6–44; "Note complementaire sur l'inspiration," *Revue biblique* 63 (1956): 416–422; "Analogies," pp. 6–35 = "Les analogies de l'inspiration," *Sacra Pagina: Miscellanea Biblica Congressus Internationalis Catholici de Re Biblica*, 2 vols., ed. Joseph Coppens, Albert Descamps, and Edouard Massaux, Bibliotheca Ephemeridum Theologicarum Lovainiensium, vols. 12–13 (Gembloux: Duculot, 1959), 1:86–99 = *Exegese et Theologie*, 3:17–30; "L'inspiration des Septante d'apres les Peres," *L'homme devant Dieu: Melanges offerts au Pere Henri de Lubac, S.J.*, 3 vols. (Paris: Aubier, 1963), 1:169–187 = *Exegese et Theologie*, 3:69–89; "Revelation and Inspiration," *Aspects*, pp. 36–127 = "Revelation et Inspiration selon la Bible, chez Saint Thomas et dan les discussions moderns," *Revue biblique* 70 (1963): 321–370 = *Exegese et* Theologie, 3:90–142; and "Inspiration," pp. 6–24. Benoit's views are summarized well by Scullion, *Theology*, pp. 36–40.

rather than an "illumination," for the latter definition could lead to the distinction between ideas and words and give rise to the debate as to whether ideas or both words and ideas are inspired (as it did in nineteenth century Roman Catholic circles). The strength of his discussion was enhanced by his ability to use traditional Thomistic categories. With this definition of inspiration Benoit described the individual as acting freely but affected by a "directive dynamism," an "impulse and orientation," a "surge of the Spirit" which leads people to act, speak, or write and thus proclaim divine truth. Furthermore, this inspiration operates in the teaching and interpreting function of the Church today as an "ecclesial inspiration" as opposed to the deeper and more profound "biblical inspiration" which produced the Scriptures.[5] (2) Biblical inspiration primarily affects "practical judgment" rather than "speculative judgment." Prophetic illumination affects cognitive abilities and brings illumination to the prophet's speculative judgment (as Lagrange had said), but the creation of Scripture involves the practical task of creating literature and choosing appropriate literary forms. The creation of Scripture involves an inspiration of the practical judgment of the author—it is a stimulation of the will and a direction of the practical judgment to speak or write. For Benoit and others this helped to clarify the distinction between revelation or illumination (speculative) and inspiration or communication (practical) and unite both functions in a coherent theological scheme.[6]

Benoit helped lay foundations for the model of social inspiration. He spoke of a collective inspiration which extended to all who formed sacred history, the prophets who formed the conscience as well as the writers who gathered the essential materials. To limit inspiration to individuals is to "impoverish to a dangerous degree the extreme riches of the encounter that God offers man in the Bible."[7] Inspiration is a "long thrust of the Spirit" through three stages: (1) dramatic/historical inspiration (cognitive) in the salvific events or history and the actions of peo-

---

5. Synave and Benoit, *Prophecy,* passim; Benoit, "Analogies," pp. 13–24, and "Revelation," pp. 77–82, 121, 126.

6. Synave and Benoit, *Prophecy,* pp. 110–117; Benoit, "Revelation," pp. 38–40; Pirot, "Inspiration," pp. 11–12; J. McKenzie, "Inspiration," p. 392; Smith, "Inspiration," pp. 507–508; and Harrington, *Record,* p. 121, and *Key to the Bible,* Vol. 1: *Record of Revelation* (Garden City: Doubleday, 1976), pp. 41, 47, who points out that many of the Thomistic categories have been abandoned subsequently.

7. Benoit, "Revelation," p. 76.

ple, (2) prophetic/apostolic inspiration (oratorical) inspiration in the impulse which directs speakers to proclaim the message, and (3) scriptural inspiration (hagiographic) which leads the writers to produce the text.[8] However, unlike the later social inspiration advocates, Benoit did not let go of stressing the importance of individuals.[9]

From a theological perspective Karl Rahner laid the foundation for social inspiration.[10] For him inspiration was a unique function of the apostolic Church, and the Scriptures were the articulation of that early community. "Scripture itself is the concrete process and the objectification of the original Church's consciousness of the faith."[11] Rahner perceived that God created the Christian community of faith, and it in turn produced the Scriptures as the literary articulation of the faith response to revelation in the resurrection of Jesus Christ. Therefore, God was the principal author of Scripture through the secondary authorship of the Church. Viewed in this perspective, the tradition making process of the apostolic Church was prior to the written Scriptures, so that tradition created Scripture. The individual inspired authors of the Bible were members of an interpersonal world which bequeathed to them the faith they expressed. The Bible is the deposit of the oral tradition produced by the apostolic Church; it is the normative objectification of the tradition of the earliest community.[12]

---

8. Synave and Benoit, *Prophecy*, p. 126; and Benoit, "Analogies," pp. 21–31, and "Inspiration," p. 17.

9. Alonso-Schökel, *Word*, p. 22, and Harrington, *Key*, p. 47, have criticized Benoit for being too artificial and too Thomistic.

10. Rahner, "Über die Schriftinspiration," *Zeitschrift für katholische Theologie* 78 (1956): 137–168, "Ecriture et Tradition a propos du schema conciliaire sur la Revelation divine," *L'homme devant Dieu*, 3:209–221, "Exegesis and Dogmatic Theology," *Dogmatic vs. Biblical Theology*, ed. Herbert Vorgrimler (Baltimore: Helicon, 1964), pp. 31–65, offers Rahner's discussion of inerrancy, pp. 31–65, *Inspiration*, pp. 6–80, *Foundations*, pp. 369–378, *Theological Investigations*, Vol. 6: *Concerning Vatican II*, trans. Karl H. and Boniface Kruger (Baltimore: Helicon, 1969), pp. 89–112; and Rahner and Joseph Ratzinger, *Revelation and Tradition*, trans. W.J. O'Hara (New York: Herder and Herder, 1966), pp. 9–25. His significant contributions in this area are evaluated by Topel, "Social Theory," pp. 33–44; Scullion, *Theology*, pp. 40–44; and Vawter, *Inspiration*, p. 111.

11. Rahner, *Foundations*, p. 376; similar statements are made on p. 372, and in *Investigations*, 6:90, 102–103, and *Inspiration*, p. 50.

12. Rahner, "Schriftinspiration," pp. 137–168, "Ecriture," pp. 209–221, *Inspiration*, pp. 39–63, and *Foundations*, pp. 158–161. Concurring with him are Harrington, *Record*, pp. 125–126; J. McKenzie, "Inspiration," p. 392; and Rupert Geiselmann, *The Meaning of Tradition*, Quaestiones Disputatae, Vol. 15 (New York: Herder and Herder, 1966), pp. 31–38.

Rahner's presentation emphasizes the distinctively Roman Catholic agenda in the social inspiration model. His concern to discuss the relationship of Scripture to tradition, so that Scripture and the magisterium are a co-terminus creation by God, reflects his theological commitment to his tradition. By the resurrection event God creates the Church which creates tradition out of which arises the Scriptures, but they in turn remain "the concrete norm for the post-apostolic Church in its future understanding of the faith."[13] This is Rahner's response to a two source theory of tradition and Scripture—he merges them into a circle; tradition creates Scripture which is the norm for later traditions. Scripture is normative for future ages because it comes from the crucial moment in the formation of the Church, the apostolic era.[14] Rahner can conclude,

> Since scripture is something derivative, it must be understood from the essential nature of the church, which is the eschatological and irreversible permanence of Jesus Christ in history. . . . Then he (God) is the inspirer and the author of scripture, although the inspiration of scripture is "only" a moment within God's primordial authorship or the church.[15]

For Rahner and those who follow him the New Testament is taken from the "apostolic deposit" of the faith—its roots must be in the apostolic era.[16] Ultimate authority lies outside the text.

There are some weaknesses in Rahner's views, which should be mentioned. His understanding is not new, for similar ideas were advanced by Johann Drey and Johann Möhler in the Tübingen school, who considered Scripture the embodiment of tradition.[17] Two problems arise with Rahner's thesis as he presents it: (1) Rahner's strong emphasis upon the apostolic period as the era of inspiration relegates the entire Old Testament to an inferior status. He posits that the Old Testament was not canon

---

13. Rahner, *Foundations*, p. 363.

14. Rahner, *Inspiration*, p. 74, *Investigations*, pp. 89–112, *Foundations*, pp. 361, 373; and Harrington, *Record*, pp. 125–126.

15. Rahner, *Foundations*, pp. 371, 375.

16. Pierre Grelot, "Tradition as Source and Environment of Scripture," trans. Theodore Westow, *The Dynamism of Biblical Tradition, Concilium*, Vol. 20 (New York: Paulist, 1967), p. 26; and James Turro and Raymond E. Brown, "Canonicity," *Jerome Biblical Commentary*, pp. 517–518.

17. Burtchaell, *Catholic Theories*, pp. 8–25; and Scullion, *Theology*, p. 24.

until the Church took it into its own canon.[18] Inspiration of the New Testament experience is denied to the Old Testament. This is his greatest weakness, for few biblical scholars can accept a model which subordinates the Old Testament in such fashion.[19] If the authority of Scripture lies in its firm anchorage in the apostolic era, then the Old Testament can have no authority, regardless of whether it was "taken up" by the New Testament canon. This view therefore implies that a major portion of the Bible lacks its own authority. How can it be then said that the Bible is authoritative as a whole for doing theology? (2) Rahner appears to have two levels of meaning for tradition. The tradition or oral proclamation of the faith in the apostolic Church (sometimes called *kerygma*) is the source from which the Scriptures arose. But there appears to be a qualitative difference between that tradition and the later development or traditions which are subordinate to the Scriptures. Though Rahner does not try to clearly distinguish between the tradition and the traditions, other theologians do (and they shall be discussed below), and such a distinction would ruin his view of the circularity of Scripture and tradition as coterminus authorities for Christians.

The model of social inspiration has been presented in its classic form by John McKenzie and others. Taking their cue from Rahner they speak of inspiration as a charism operative during the apostolic era as long as there was a "living memory of the experience of the incarnate Word, Jesus Christ."[20] This charism of inspiration worked within the community of faith to influence the entire process of developing Scripture, and it functioned in different ways for different types of literature. God thus worked through the community to affect individuals and produce the Scripture. This corporate inspiration is not nebulous, however, for it leads to particular insights and formulations through the individuals.[21] Even though individuals may have been used, it is not appropriate to limit inspiration to them, any more than one should limit inspiration to the mere written books. McKenzie, in particular, affirms that inspiration must extend to the entire community, for the individual author was merely "a

---

18. Rahner, *Inspiration*, pp. 51–54.

19. Vawter, *Inspiration*, p. 112.

20. J. McKenzie, "The Social Character of Inspiration," *Myths and Realities: Studies in Biblical Theology* (Milwaukee: Bruce, 1963), p. 69 = *Catholic Biblical Quarterly* 24 (1962): 115–124.

21. Ibid., p. 68; McCarthy, "Personality," p. 574; and Vawter, *Inspiration*, pp. 158–170.

spokesman of the society for which and in which he spoke."[22] For McKenzie the individual was submerged in the group, and thus cannot be rightfully described as "inspired" in isolated fashion.

> . . . the ancient author was anonymous because he did not think of himself as an individual speaker, as the modern author does. He was anonymous because in writing he fulfilled a social function; through him the society of which he was a member wrote its thoughts. . . . The modern author is an artist who feels a compulsion to express his individuality through his art; the ancient writer, if we can judge from what he wrote, was more interested in concealing his individuality. He wished to be the voice of Israel and of the Church, to produce in writing utterances which were not the expression of his own mind but of his society.[23]

The biblical traditions are more than the sum of individual expressions; they are a collection of the entire community of faith. Furthermore, if an individual writer was deficient in knowledge he or she would be led to consult the faith and traditions of the community, the true source of salvific memories. Inspiration is social and communal because the sacred authors cannot be separated from their community. The author has an experience of the divine, which arises in the communal worship life; it is not necessarily a message from God which leads the author to create Scripture. The authors of Sacred Scripture drew upon the traditions of the community to create their work; they did their theologizing as representatives of the community, and the work they produced was designed to edify the community.[24] McKenzie paraphrases Rahner when he says that the authors of the New Testament books "wrote them as officers and representatives of the Church which is the real author of the New Testament."[25]

A variation of this position is the view presented by Norbert Lohfink. He speaks of the canon as inspired and inerrant only in its totality or final

22. J. McKenzie, "Inspiration," p. 392.

23. J. McKenzie, "Social Character," pp. 64–65.

24. Ibid., pp. 66–67; Grelot, "Tradition," p. 15; Smith, "Inspiration," pp. 508–509; and Barr, *Scope*, pp. 124–125.

25. J. McKenzie, "Social Character," p. 64.

form. Each layer of Scripture was an interpretation of a previous layer, and each reinterpretation brought out the "fuller meaning" (*sensus plenior*) of the earlier text. Each part of the Bible is incomplete until the final level of reinterpretation—the New Testament interprets the Old Testament. With the completion of the canon the final interpretation is finished and closed forever. Every part has authority only in the light of the whole. Lohfink stresses the communality of the biblical tradition and the communal origin in a way that has brought him favorable consideration from those sympathetic to social inspiration.[26]

The strengths of the social inspiration theory are manifold. Grace is mediated to people, not to the books or through the written word, but rather directly to the people for whom salvation was intended.[27] This eliminates the idea of the scriptural mediation of grace and the risk of bibliolatry.

If inspiration is attributed to the group, the distinction between inspiration and revelation is blurred. McKenzie views this as an advantage, since the old theories often had to make artificial distinctions: revelation was experienced by the author and inspiration was a quality of the book. The latter distinction could easily develop into some model of understanding the Bible to be a corpus of revealed propositional truths. This model prevents us from limiting inspiration as an attribute of a book and from trying to make an artificial separation between revelation and inspiration.[28]

The social theory appeals not only to Bible scholars but to the modern mind in general, for it speaks in sociological categories which have become part of our modern intellectual heritage. We view individuals not only as distinct entities but as members of their society and as products of their environment. This theory understands and uses that conceptual apparatus.

Such a model theologically understands the cultural context of the Scriptures. The world view, social values, and sometimes limited perspectives of the biblical text are merely a reflection of the community of

---

26. Lohfink, "The Inerrancy and the Unity of Scripture," *Modern Biblical Studies,* pp. 31–42 = "Über die Irrtumlosigkeit und die Einheit der Schrift," *Stimmen der Zeit* 174 (1964): 31–42; Joseph Coppens, "Comment mieux concevoir et enoncer l'inspiration et l'inerrance des Saintes Ecritures," *Nouvelle Revue Theologique* 86 (1964): 947; and Vawter, *Inspiration,* pp. 148–150.

27. Rahner, *Foundations,* p. 370.

28. J. McKenzie, "Social Character," pp. 67–68.

faith and the values at that time. As pilgrim people whom God is leading toward a fuller self-realization, their imperfections can be accepted by modern readers.[29]

The old debate over degrees of inspiration is finally put to rest. Certain parts of the canon were perceived as more relevant for the theological task, and the question arose as to whether they were more inspired. However, if we view the community as inspired, the question of degrees of inspiration no longer applies to the various works.[30] Rather we might speak of degrees of enduring theological relevance.

This model avoids the pitfalls of the mantic model of prophecy. No longer is the author seen as a person seized by the deity, or as a mouthpiece of the deity. Rather the author of the Scripture is seen as a theologian speaking on behalf of the community of faith and to that community.

Modern biblical scholarship has impressed upon us the awareness that Scripture is produced by a number of individuals. The old model of inspiration has difficulty answering the question of whom to attribute the charism of inspiration. This was especially the case with anonymous and pseudynomous works, and to a lesser extent included glosses or additions to the text. Led by a model of individual inspiration, scholars would often excise those passages considered to be secondary additions to the text to obtain the more original text which went back to the first inspired speaker. Now the entire text may be considered relevant for the theological task, because the entire text is a product of the inspired community of faith. Bards, prophets, historiographers, redactors, scribes, and all connected with the creation of the text are subsumed together with the believing community under the gift of divine inspiration. This avoids the temptation to consider either the final writers to be inspired, as with verbal inspiration theories, or the first prophetic spokespersons alone to be inspired, as with liberal Protestant theories.[31]

The biblical research of the past two centuries has also impressed upon us how the creation of Scripture was a process of developing traditions. How can one speak of an inspired process of developing traditions and then relate that to a model of individual inspiration? It can be done

---

29. Johnston, *Evangelicals,* p. 45.
30. J. McKenzie, "Social Character," pp. 67–68.
31. Ibid, pp. 62–63; and Lohfink, "Inerrancy," pp. 31–42.

only artificially by declaring that all the individuals were inspired singularly. But that raises the question of degrees of inspiration according to the function of each individual. The model of individual inspiration becomes cumbersome at that point. Social inspiration avoids the problems by seeking the locus in the group.[32]

Certain criticisms have been raised against this theory, however—several of them by proponents of the theory who object to McKenzie's particularly strong emphasis upon the communal aspect. The chief criticism of McKenzie's understanding is that he underplays the importance of the individual. Even if it can be said that inspiration was an attribute of the entire community, the contributions of significant individuals cannot be overlooked.[33] McKenzie's view "spreads inspiration thin," and renders the concept vague and amorphous. A piece of literature is not produced by "everybody"; particular individuals create it. Even if they represent the beliefs of the group, their particular service in articulating the faith will set them apart from the rest of the community.[34]

McKenzie's view overlooks the creative advance brought about by gifted individuals. If the literature merely reflects the beliefs of the group, how do new ideas and insights arise? Do we not postulate that a gifted individual can put the old traditions together in a new way so as to promote theological growth? The traditio-historical development of material in the text implies a growth process which can be better attributed to insightful theologians rather than the group as a whole. The various prophets, the Yahwist, Paul, and other individuals seem to stand forth as markedly individual personalities.[35]

McKenzie's model overlooks the role of dissent in the development of Scripture. The Book of Job challenges the traditional values of wisdom literature and Deuteronomy. It is a religious masterpiece, in part because it challenges existing orthodoxy and opens up new insights for the audience. Job does not conform to the model of Scripture reflecting the community's values. Paul was the dissenter of his age, especially in his

32. J. McKenzie, "Social Character," pp. 60–63.
33. Benoit, "Analogies," pp. 24–26; McCarthy, "Personality," pp. 553–576; Smith, "Inspiration," p. 510; Heidt, *Introduction*, pp. 14–15; Vawter, *Inspiration*, pp. 158–159; and Harrington, *Key*, pp. 47–49.
34. Alonso-Schökel, *Word*, p. 224; and Scullion, *Thelogy*, p. 45.
35. McCarthy, "Personality," p. 572; and Scullion, *Theology*, pp. 46–49.

opposition to the Judaizers. A social model begins to attribute inspiration to all involved, including the Judaizers. Obviously the intent of Scripture or the Pauline letters is to affirm the priority of Paul's position in the apostolic community. Many biblical books were not the product of a community, but the work of individuals reacting against popular values. The books arose from "the repeated, centuries-long confrontation by individuals raised up to denounce the infidelity and immorality of the social group."[36] The model of social inspiration can give validation to the syncretistic practices which may have arisen in the communities of faith, as well as popular and bizarre beliefs which were never part of the normative developing faith.

Traditions in the Bible appear to emphasize the importance of the individual's relationship to God at times. Though the prophets were rooted in their Mosaic traditions, they experienced a personal encounter with God and they were set apart by a call experience. The emphasis upon the special nature of such a call to be a spokesperson for God appears to counter any denial of the individual's importance. The biblical tradition does not seem to give a direct affirmation of the social model of group inspiration; rather the group always seems to be addressed or led by a chosen individual.[37]

Some literature in the Bible is taken from the ancient Near Eastern milieu of Israel or the Graeco-Roman world of early Christianity. Is this material the product of an inspired community? The social inspiration model cannot deal with literature which arises outside the community of faith. In particular, the Old Testament wisdom literature is ignored, for it is part of the universal literary and intellectual tradition of the ancient world.[38]

This model fails to perceive the literary character of Scripture—it is art. Literature is produced by creative individuals, not the masses. "There is no such thing as a literary work produced by 'everybody,' and there is no need to revive the romantic theory which dissolved a work of art back into the masses."[39]

A number of McKenzie's critics, however, are impressed by the

36. Heidt, *Introduction*, p. 15.
37. McCarthy, "Personality," pp. 556–558; and ibid., p. 16.
38. McCarthy, "Personality," p. 573; and Smith, "Inspiration," p. 510.
39. Alonso-Schökel, *Word*, p. 224.

basic model of social inspiration and seek to use it in conjunction with an emphasis upon the importance of the individual. Individuals still did the work of creating the literature, even if they were anonymous. All literature involves a subtle interplay of the individual and the cultural tradition from which he or she emerged. The community relies upon and benefits from gifted individuals who direct its destiny. Social inspiration is a charism shared by many individuals in the community, but to a greater or lesser extent for each of them.[40] According to Benoit inspiration "illuminates and directs a structured society through individuals chosen and personally endowed with charisms to serve the group."[41]

This newer revised position meets the challenges and avoids the problems posed to the classic social inspiration theory of McKenzie. However, it has to face the return of earlier criticism leveled against advocates of individual inspiration: (1) Are there levels of inspiration among the individuals? Benoit would say yes, and affirm this as the basis for distinctions among ecclesiastical leaders in the current Church.[42] Few would accept the implications of Benoit's statement, for the creators of Scripture were not leaders of the structured Church (Paul was at odds with James, the more "official" hierarchy in the ancient Church). Even today theologians and biblical exegetes are seldom in positions of ecclesiastical leadership. (2) We must again raise the related question concerning degrees of inspiration among the canonical books. Are certain works more inspired than others because they come from truly inspired individuals like Paul and the prophets? (3) How do we understand the process of creating Scripture? Are certain individuals in the process more inspired than others? If so, which are they: the molders of oral tradition or the creative editors and redactors? Thus any attempt to modify the classic social model of McKenzie will face challenging questions of its own.

The model of social inspiration is a good model, for it appears to have a greater sensitivity to the biblical text. The emphasis upon the group or community of faith reflects biblical agenda more than previous models

---

40. Yves Congar, "Inspiration des ecritures canoniques et apostolicite de l'Eglise," *Revue des Sciences Philosophiques et Theologiques* 45 (1961): 32–42; Benoit, "Inspiration," p. 16; and McCarthy, "Personality," p. 554.

41. Synave and Benoit, *Prophecy*, p. 127.

42. Ibid.

of inspiration which emphasized individual inspiration exclusively. The strongest criticisms against social inspiration have come from within the ranks of advocates rather than from outside critics.[43] As a fairly recent model the social theory of inspiration may have a future in scholarly circles, if more scholars begin to use and develop the ideas (especially if it moves beyond the present circle of Roman Catholic theologians).

---

43 Montgomery, "The Approach of New Shape Roman Catholicism to Scriptural Inerrancy: A Case Study" *God's Inerrant Word*, pp. 263–281, criticizes the model completely, but his arguments are extremely bitter, naive, and ineffective.

Chapter Eight

INSPIRATION IN RETROSPECT

A great amount of time has been spent with models which emphasize inspiration. This is appropriate, because throughout the greater Christian tradition the appeal to undergird the concept of authority has often been to inspiration.

This study hopefully has revealed the great diversity of opinion on the concept of inspiration. This diversity reflects not only the natural inclination of theologians to disagree and to move in diverse directions with their articulations; more importantly it reflects the paucity of clarification to be found in the biblical text about inspiration. In a few scattered places inspiration is claimed as an attribute of the Scriptures, but little more than that is said.

Theories of inspiration all have certain weaknesses inherent in them.

If they speak of the material as being delivered or inspired by God, they have to answer the question to what extent is the text divine and/or human. This immediately raises questions of certitude and accuracy. Some theories boldly define the diversity and accuracy of the text, while others seek to define inspiration in a way so as to allow difficult passages to fall harmlessly to the side. But in order to avoid all the problems, inspiration may be defined so narrowly that it no longer applies to the text. Then it no longer addresses the question of biblical authority.

Working with the model of inspiration, theologians are tempted to argue whether those parts of Scripture which are more meaningful for theology are more inspired. This is natural if we connect inspiration to authority. If we view a text as more authoritative for our theology, we are tempted to view it as more inspired, or inspired with a deeper quality than other texts. This is a problem of misplaced categories.

Our modern understanding of the developmental process in the creation of the biblical text renders traditional models of inspiration naive. How can we speak of an inspired Scripture when so many people were involved in creating the text? Only those theories which speak of inspiration as an attribute of the original speaker or of the community as a whole seek to address this problem.

Some modern theories which try to explain the process of inspiration in a workable fashion for theology are artificial. Some try to limit inspiration to ideas, and that is psychologically and linguistically unsound. Others try to explain the mental process in Thomistic categories, and though they seem logical, they are very hypothetical and contingent upon certain philosophical presuppositions. The best conclusion is uttered by Richard Smith:

> . . . the psychology of the human writer under the influence of inspiration escapes us, and probably always will. In itself the process of composing a written document is an obscure one; and under the influence of inspiration, that process can only be more obscure.[1]

Inspiration theories often appeal to Christology for analogy. Just as Jesus was human and divine, so Scripture is human and divine. What happens so often, however, is that the theologizing about the Bible affects one's Christology. Strict verbal inspirationists tend to overemphasize the divinity of both. The analogy between Jesus Christ and the Bible is not appropriate, for Christ is said to be totally human and totally divine, two natures in one personal union. When we speak of Scripture the personal union language is not available. We may speak of Scripture as totally divine and totally human in theory, but in practice we really speak of the interaction of two dynamic aspects—God and the human author. We speak of interaction in describing inspiration but not when we speak of Jesus Christ. The analogy breaks down at the point where we need it.

For these reasons the concept of authority may best be defined apart from the category of inspiration. Authority is the prior category. Inspiration is a corollary; it is subordinate. Because the Bible is authoritative, we may speak of it as inspired. (It is the icing on the cake!) Inspiration is a second order doctrine. Inspiration describes a quality of the text, but

---

1. Smith, "Inspiration," p. 509.

the concept of authority seeks to describe why the Scriptures should be used. The reason for authority should also explicate how Scripture ought concretely to be used and understood in the life of the Church and in the doing of theology. Inspiration does not do that. It merely tells us why the Scriptures were effective once we used them under the mandate of biblical authority. (It is for this reason that a World Council of Churches report at Louvain in 1971 chose to discuss the authority of the Bible not from the perspective of its inspiration, but from its religious value for the Church.)[2] We must look elsewhere to understand the basis for biblical authority.

---

2. Kelsey, *Scripture*, pp. 210–211; Dulles, "Scripture: Recent Protestant and Catholic Views," *Authoritative Word*, p. 246 = *Theology Today* 37 (1980): 7–26; Johnston, *Evangelicals*, p. 5; and Hoffman, "Sacred Character," pp. 450–451.

Chapter Nine

SALVATION HISTORY

Among Bible scholars in the twentieth century a new model arose for understanding the central message of the Bible and the locus of its authority. They viewed the Bible as an account of salvific events rather than ideational or propositional revelation. The German word *Heilsge-schichte* which means "holy history" or "salvation history" has been associated with various individuals who tend to use this model.

Heilsgeschichte models attempt to be more sensitive to the biblical modes of thought. Among biblical theologians in recent years it has been customary to view the Bible as a record of the saving events initiated by God for his people, a record of events by which God delivered, saved, constituted, and preserved his holy people, be they Israel or the Christian Church. Paramount events are the exodus and the resurrection of Jesus; both events are viewed as irruptions into human history by a gracious God on behalf of a helpless people.

Within the movement three subdivisions may be noted. Most advocates would point to the salvific events as the source of authority, while others more cautiously affirm the interpretation of the events by the biblical theologians to be the source of authority, and a few would affirm radically that history is itself the revelation of God and the important structure of divine-human relations.

SALVIFIC EVENTS AS AUTHORITATIVE

George Ernest Wright, Reginald Fuller, Oscar Cullman, John Bright, Paul Minear, and many others would affirm the basic position briefly outlined above. They would declare that God has acted decisively in the exodus and resurrection, that Scripture bears testimony to these events, and that the continued repetition of this salvific activity by God is rooted in the once and for all nature of those primal events. The community of faith is created by those events and looks back to those events for self-understanding. Traditions develop around the events and theological articulation turns to them as the norm for the faith. God reveals himself in history; the Bible is the record of that self-revelation and the only source for divine self-disclosure. It is not primarily the word of God; rather it is the record of divine actions in history. God is known by what he has done, and the divine attributes are inferred from these actions. The divine actions are a subset of events in human history, not the human history as a whole. Undergirding this is a promise of continued future activities of a gracious God on our behalf.[1]

In the modern era the Bible is seen as having little authority. Advocates of this position desire to present the Bible in categories the modern mind can understand and affirm. The historical consciousness of modern people is open to such a new interpretation. In this model the authority of the Bible is derived from the events to which it testifies. The faith of Israel and Christianity are deeply rooted in a theology of history, and proponents declare this to be a liberation from religious movements based on myth, inner experience, and philosophical speculation.[2] Scripture has authority today because it testifies to the events of the exodus and the resurrection and brings them to life for today's readers.

Such a position has many strengths. Priority is placed upon the key events recorded in the Bible rather than upon the Bible as a book. Errors in the text pose no problem for the reader, since they do not affect the central message; they only reflect the imperfections of the human wit-

---

1. Dodd, *Authority*, pp. 9, 216–219, 257–263, 273, and "The Relevance of the Bible," *Symposium*, p. 160; Norman Snaith, *The Inspiration and Authority of the Bible* (London: Epworth, 1956), pp. 9–46; George Ernest Wright, *God Who Acts: Biblical Theology as Recital*, Studies in Biblical Theology, Vol. 8 (London: SCM, 1952), pp. 12–13, 15–32, 107, and "From the Bible to the Modern World," *Symposium*, pp. 219–239; Wright and Reginald Fuller, *The Book of the Acts of God*, Christian Faith Series, ed. Reinhold Niebuhr (Garden City: Doubleday, 1957), pp. 27–33; Bratsiotis, "Orthodox Contribution," pp. 17–29, Vinjamuri Devadutt, "A Baptist Contribution," pp. 59–81, Georges Florovsky, "Revelation and Interpretation," pp. 163–180, James Muilenburg, "The Interpretation of the Bible," pp. 198–218, and throughout the other articles in *Symposium*, passim; Richardson, *The Bible in the Age of Science* (Philadelphia: Westminster, 1961), pp. 122–141, provides a good summary of Dodd, Cullmann, and Wright; and Kelsey, *Scripture*, pp. 33–35, analyzes the movement.

2. Wright, *God Who Acts*, pp. 12–32, 107; and Gordon Kaufman, "What Shall We Do with the Bible?" *Interpretation* 25 (1971): 95–112.

nesses to the divine events.[3] Nor is the exegete bound to accept the world view of the biblical authors, for as Cullmann states, the redemptive framework is important, not the world view.[4] This avoids the dilemma of the fundamentalist. With the historical model one can admit to some form of religious development or progressive revelation which ultimately culminates in the ministry of Jesus. Thus the primitive morality exhibited in some parts of Scripture may be excused as steps along the way to the ultimate revelation.[5] Past allegorical interpretation dealt with such difficult passages only in an inadequate fashion, but now the modern thought category of historical development enables us to move beyond such passages so that the text may speak to us more authoritatively.[6]

There are some problems with this model, however. We must elevate the intellectual category of history to a level of importance that the ancient Hebrews and Christians would not have given it. Their concept of history is not ours, for they lacked notions of progress, process, objectivity, and facticity in reporting. They even lacked a particular word for history. Stretching the use of our modern word to fit their view of reality renders the word meaningless.[7]

More problematic for the exegete is that the *Heilsgeschichte* construct cannot account for all the literature in the Bible. Wisdom literature in the Old and New Testaments betrays no real awareness of a God who acts in history; rather it is concerned with the order in the universe, the relationship of human deeds and their results, and the way in which people may live in their everyday society. Wisdom categories are didactic and experiential, akin to philosophy rather than redemptive historical categories. The Psalms are cultic material with a doxological emphasis which only rarely relies on *Heilsgeschichte* themes. God is praised as Creator and Preserver rather than as Redeemer who acts in history. Furthermore, the model cannot deal with the aspect of the direct and personal encounter with the divine, which the Hebrews considered most important. The con-

3. Dodd, *Authority,* p. 241.

4. Oscar Cullmann, *Christ and Time,* trans. Floyd Filson (Philadelphia: Westminster, 1964), pp. 13, 96.

5. Richardson, "Biblical Scholarship," pp. 302–303; and Bright, *Authority,* pp. 188–189.

6. Dodd, *Authority,* p. 183; and Barr, "The Interpretation of Scripture. II. Revelation Through History in the Old Testament and Modern Theology," *Interpretation* 17 (1963): 200–202.

7. Barr, "Interpretation," pp. 197–199.

frontation of Moses by God on the mountain of Sinai is a timeless and universal experience which leaves the historical elements in the background. The personal communion experienced by the prophets with God, including the tremendous impact of their call experiences, moves into personal and timeless categories. The universal imperative of the law, especially the Decalogue, lacks the historicality of any given situation. Nor can the direct relationship with the Father of which Jesus speaks, nor the experience of Paul in encountering the risen Lord, be made to fit comfortably within the *Heilsgeschichte* framework. They appear to have an intensely personal and timeless quality about them.

There remains a philosophical problem. The biblical text is neither scientific history nor even an accurate report of the events; rather it contains theologically directed mythic and epic interpretations. The authoritative events lack access, and how can we declare them to be historical events when our sources are not, properly speaking, "historical"? The advocates of this position do not really open the Bible up for genuine critical and empirical observation, for that is impossible. Thus the Bible is not really authoritative, only the events are, and if we have no access to the events as we have defined them, we have no authority left.[8]

These theologians have not dealt with the ramification of using the construct of history. They fail to demonstrate the connection between holy history and universal human history. They have created a special meta-history outside of normal historical categories. Furthermore, they do not explain how an event can contain divine revelation. One must still perceive who God is and how he is behind the event. There must occur some form of interpretation, for brute facts of history are not revelation. The Bible implies that God must speak to prophets and apostles. The relationship between history and revelation is not thoroughly developed.[9]

This position actually appears to limit divine grace in a new fashion rather than liberate it. Wright and others reject treating Scripture in the static categories of inspiration, for they are too conceptual. However, these advocates enclose Scripture with a new conceptual category, history. Divine grace is limited to historical and spatial categories.[10]

---

8. Barr, *Bible,* pp. 75–88; and Kelsey, "Protestant Attitudes," p. 159.

9. Kelsey, *Scripture,* pp. 37–38; Carl F. Henry, *God, Revelation and Authority,* Vol. 2: *God Who Speaks and Shows* (Waco: Word, 1976), pp. 281–293; and Abraham, *Holy Scripture,* pp. 76–90.

10. Kelsey, *Scripture,* p. 37, and "Protestant Attitudes," p. 159.

INTERPRETATION OF THE EVENTS AS SALVIFIC

Difficulties with the relationship between actual human history and the category of salvific events are apparent to more philosophically and theologically reflective individuals in this movement. For this reason several scholars have been reluctant to point to the events as an ultimate source of authority.

This historical event (*historie*) is a nebulous inascertainable thing, but what we have is an interpretation of history (*geschichte*). An event is meaningless until it is interpreted by the eye of faith. The text before us contains "interpretations of historical events" or "projections from known events" which were created in the faith process of early Israel and the ancient Church. Interpretation is more important than the history, and the Bible is seen as a faith response to events.[11] In fact, the historicity of the events is unimportant, and the interpretation may remake the event so as to render it unrecognizable to the critical historian. Advocates like Gerhard von Rad and Rudolf Bultmann would consider much of the Bible to be faith interpretation of events with little or no historicity. The original event can never be rediscovered, and its rediscovery is unimportant. History is swallowed up by faith as reason bows to faith, and the interpretation of the events carries the true meaning and authority for us today.[12]

This position honestly admits the gap between the ancient mind and ours; the existence of historical lacunae, inconsistencies, and contradictions in the text poses no problem for the theologian. No quest for the historical Jesus or Moses is necessary to find the seat of authority or the kernel of the Christian religion as nineteenth century theologians felt constrained to do. Rather it accepts the subjective faith interpretation in the

---

11. Wright and Fuller, *Book*, pp. 21–23; Wright, *God, Who Acts*, p. 11; Austin Farrar, *The Glass of Vision* (London: n.p., 1948), passim, which repeats thoughts from his 1948 Bampton Lectures; and Richardson, "Biblical Scholarship," p. 334.

12. Von Rad, *Old Testament Theology*, 2 vols., trans. Stalker (New York: Harper and Row, 1962), 1:106 et passim, and "The Form Critical Problem of the Hexateuch," *The Problem of the Hexateuch and Other Essays*, trans. Trueman Dicken (New York: McGraw-Hill, 1966), pp. 1–78; Rudolph Bultmann, *Theology of the New Testament*, trans. Kenrick Grobel (New York: Scribner's, 1951, 1955), pp. 33–53 et passim, and *Jesus Christ and Mythology* (New York: Scribner's, 1958), pp. 35–58 et passim; Bright, *Authority*, p. 148; and Bryant, *Authority*, p. 41.

text without concern for historicity. The scholar can be merciless in his or her criticism, and the work remains positive. For the chaff of history falls aside so that faith might arise. This reflects a strong north European distinction between the power of faith and reason, and most advocates of this viewpoint come from that theological milieu. They are faithful to their denominations' theological presuppositions.

The weaknesses can be great. Solipsism may ensue as the gap between event and text widens. We may be placing faith in a fabrication, a distortion of history, and this remains an unsettling possibility for defenders of this viewpoint. Since there is no stress on the historic norm, the subjectivity in interpretation arises with the interpreter's freedom to reinterpret the material for the modern existential situation. This is best demonstrated by Bultmann's existential interpretation of the New Testament *kerygma* in Heideggerian categories. The historical image of Jesus may be lost in the theological scheme which becomes the more important message. Ultimately all such theological constructs can be rationalistic, and biblical data which do not fit the pattern are ignored or reinterpreted to fit the theology. Often typology can be used to modify uncomfortable biblical data.[13] This position always runs the risk of elevating the theology of the interpreter over the message of the text.

HISTORY AS REVELATION

A third position among biblical theologians seeks to move the locus of authority from the biblical text to the arena of history itself. Wolfhart Pannenberg, Jürgen Moltmann, Rolf Rendtorff, Trutz Rendtorff, Ulrich Wilkins, and others declare that God does more than reveal himself in history; rather history itself is revelation, and as such it is the continuing sphere of divine self-disclosure in our own age.[14] These theologians have

---

13. W. Schweitzer, "Biblical Theology," pp. 144–146.

14. Wolfhart Pannenberg, "Hermeneutics and Universal History," trans. Paul Achtemeier, *History and Hermeneutic,* Journal for Theology and the Church, Vol. 4, eds. Robert Funk and Gerhard Ebeling (New York: Harper and Row, 1967), pp. 122–125, "Heilsgeschehen und Geschichte," *Kerygma und Dogma* 5 (1959): 218–237, 259–288, and "Die Aufnahme des philosophischen Gottesbegriff als dogmatisches Problem der frühchristlichen Theologie," *Zeitschrift für Kirchengeschichte* 70 (1959): 1–45; Ulrich Wilkens, "Die Bekehrung des Paulus als religionsgeschichtliches Problem," *Zeitschrift*

devoured the forbidden fruit and affirmed history as the authoritative category for Christian theology rather than the mere report of divine activity in history. Revelation takes place in history, not in any "subset" of events. God will be revealed ultimately at the end of history, and the totality of prior history will then be seen as part of the divine plan. Events need not be interpreted, because they carry their revelatory meaning with them. Events are part of a tradition, which is integral to those events. Pannenberg uses the philosophical categories of Gadamer to appropriate the meaning of the biblical text; since the history cannot be relived, it must be existentially reinterpreted.[15] Because of the hermeneutical distance between the interpreter and the event, the theologian must turn to the present reality of historical experience as a source for theology.

This bold new position avoids the problem of reconciling text and history, and it fears not the solipsism of subscribing to mere interpretation found in the text. Instead of viewing the exodus and the resurrection as meta-historical events, it places the holy events back into history. For it affirms God's reality in the historical process and looks to the future for new divine direction. In so doing a feel for the living Spirit who directs the Church is affirmed.[16]

This new approach unfortunately discards the canon as authority.

für Theologie und Kirche 56 (1959): 273–293, and *Die Missionrede der Apostelgeschichte,* Wissenschaftliche Monographien zum Alten und Neuen Testament, Vol. 5 (Neukirchen: Moers, 1961), passim, Rolf Rendtorff, "Hermeneutik des Alten Testaments als Frage nach Geschichte," *Zeitschrift für Theologie und Kirche* 57 (1960): 27–40, and R. Rendtorff and Klaus Koch, eds., *Studien zur Theologie der alttestamentlichen Überlieferungen: Gerhard von Rad zum 60. Geburtstag* (Neukirchen: Moers, 1961), passim; Koch, "Die Eigenart der priesterschriften Sinaigesetzgebung," *Zeitschrift für Theologie und Kirche* 55 (1958): 36–51; Dietrich Rössler, *Gesetz und Geschichte,* Wissenschaftliche Monographien zum Alten und Neuen Testament, Vol. 3 (Neukirchen: Moers, 1960), passim; Martin Elze, *Tatian und seine Theologie,* Forschungen zur Kirchen- und Dogmengeschichte, Vol. 9 (Göttingen: Vandenhoeck und Ruprecht, 1960), passim; and Jurgen Moltmann, *Theology of Hope,* trans. James Leitch (New York: Harper and Row, 1975), pp. 15–338. The most significant articulations of this position have appeared in a collection of essays, R. Rendtorff, "The Concept of Revelation in Ancient Israel," pp. 25–53, Wilkens, "The Understanding of Revelation Within the History of Primitive Christianity," pp. 57–121, Pannenberg, "Dogmatic Theses on the Doctrine of Revelation," pp. 125–158, and Trutz Rendtorff, "The Problem of Revelation in the Concept of the Church," pp. 161–181, *Revelation as History,* trans. David Granskou (New York; Macmillan, 1968), pp. 23–181. This view was implied by Dodd, *Authority,* p. 240, who spoke of history being divine revelation.

15. Pannenberg, "Hermeneutic," pp. 90–121; and a good assessment is provided by Kelsey, *Scripture,* p. 53.

16. Henry, *God,* pp. 294–295, 309.

Scripture is excluded as revelation, for it is a book, and only history is revelation. Some material which is in Scripture cannot come into any consideration, because it is not historical. Wisdom literature and psalmic material are excluded from the category of revelation because they lack the identity of history.[17]

The Bible is a guideline to describe past revelation, but the authoritative reality is seen in the present and the future. This enables theologians to avoid the problem of historical and empirical criticism merely by projecting the locus of authority into the future. The problems are avoided, not solved.[18]

Now a new subjectivity arises. How can history be a religious authority? Who will interpret it? Can a new theology now modify the old faith into a totally new reality? What are the restraining norms from any given theology of revolution, spiritual or political, which seeks to restructure the old faith? The weakness herein is the complete openness to radical new change. Though the advocates might praise such openness, would they feel comfortable with the plethora of cults that could develop with theological priorities other than their own?

This theory is preoccupied with history. The whole method makes historiography the basis for theology. Certainty for faith must be forfeit without solid historiographical principles, and for Pannenberg in particular a degree of historiographical verification must be possible. Our theological task is turned into the historian's craft.[19]

Finally, criticism has been leveled at the confusion between historical and existential categories found within the writings of these theologians. They imbue the historical dimension of reality with existential categories of moral imperative and religious response. Historical categories cannot be made to bear that weight and be used for moral, ethical, and theological purposes.[20]

To affirm history as revelation is a bold task, but perhaps a little too dangerous. Above all it leaves behind the Scriptures as a source of authority, and thus creates more problems than it solves.

17. Loretz, *Truth,* pp. 22–52.

18. Henry, *God,* pp. 294–310.

19. Loretz, *Truth,* pp. 43–52; and Henry, *God,* pp. 294–310.

20. Lothar Steiger, "Revelation-History and Theological Reason: A Critique of the Theology of Wolfhart Pannenberg," trans. Joseph Weber, *History and Hermeneutic,* pp. 82–106.

CONCLUSION

While *Heilsgeschichte* models are popular with biblical scholars and rooted in the text, they have their weaknesses. None of the models will work consistently to provide a sound basis for authority on which the community of faith may rely. Even among some biblical theologians the model has fallen into disrepute for its inability to explain all that occurs in the text. The movement has failed to offer a relevant message to the Church which unites the themes of the biblical witness while maintaining the integrity to both the text and relevant theological issues of today.[21] The very idea that the Bible has authority because it points to authoritative salvific events is self-contradictory, and the Bible then loses its claim to authority.

---

21. Brevard Childs, *Biblical Theology in Crisis* (Philadelphia: Westminster, 1970), pp. 13–87.

Chapter Ten

EXISTENTIALISM

Existential models are used to move the locus of authority from either the text or the category of history. Authority is meaningless apart from the individual who responds to it. Authority exists only when an individual is confronted, accepts, and responds to the written or preached word in his or her life situation. The past becomes relevant when brought to life in the context of faith.

This existential mode of perceiving authority takes different forms in the modern era. The most well known approach is that of Karl Barth, Emil Brunner, Friedrich Gogarten, and other dialectical neo-orthodox theologians, and the Heideggerian existentialists of Bultmann's school. Another form of interpretation which is less clearly identifiable with any theological movement perceives the text as literature capable of affecting our behavior. The symbolic aspect of the biblical narrative makes its impact upon our aesthetic and moral sensitivities according to various proponents of this understanding. A third form of existential interpretation is probably the most common and the least defined theologically. Many preachers and teachers perceive the biblical text as authoritative when it addresses existential life situations parallel to the ones in which they find themselves. Advocates of this view might not even use the term "existential," but their approach to the Bible parallels other more formal existential models.

CLASSIC EXISTENTIALISM

The concept of existential interpretation has commonly been associated with leading European theologians after World War I. The formal theological movement has been called neo-orthodoxy, dialectical theology, and crisis theology. Two leading names have been associated with the concept of existential interpretation, or the theology of personal encounter. Karl Barth, who is often viewed as the founder of the neo-orthodox movement, and Rudolf Bultmann, who is really outside that movement though he shares many characteristics with it, offer the two leading models of existential interpretation.[1]

Karl Barth has devoted a great amount of thought and writing to the idea of biblical authority.[2] His significant insight that the word of God is not to be equated with the Bible has elicited much response, favorable and critical.[3]

For Barth the word of God in its highest form is Jesus Christ. What we call the word of God are those things which bring us closer to Jesus Christ, and this includes not only the Scriptures but the proclaimed word, the *viva vox,* or the preaching and teaching of the Church. The written Scripture is not revelation or the word of God by itself; it is an instrument in the hands of God which becomes the word of God through preaching. The Scriptures are only secondarily a form of God's word.[4]

The humanity of the Bible is emphasized by Barth in order to bring out this concept. Barth rejects the idea of infallibility as a form of Bible idolatry which infringes upon the sovereignty of God; he calls this the "inscripturation of God." The Bible must be viewed as fallible or vulnerable to place God, and Jesus Christ as the word of God, in the center of theology.[5] Inspiration is not a quality of the text, but a testimony to God's ability to use the text as an occasion for a divine-human encounter. The ordinary words of a human text may then become the word of God.[6]

The authority of Scripture lies in its function, not in an inherent quality or attribute, such as inspiration, infallibility, or inerrancy. Scripture

---

1. Richardson, *Science,* pp. 100–121, offers a good evaluation of both theologians and their contributions to this hermeneutical perspective.

2. K. Barth, *Church Dogmatics,* Vol. 1, pt. 1, 47–292, and pt. 2, 457–740.

3. Alexander Jones, "Biblical Inspiration: A Christian Rendezvous?" *Scripture* 10 (1958): 97–109; Richardson, *Science,* pp. 100–121; Runia, *Doctrine,* pp. 1–219; and Rogers and McKim, *Authority,* pp. 406–426.

4. K. Barth, *Church Dogmatics,* Vol. 1, pt. 2, 457, 530 and 522–544 in general; Richardson, *Science,* pp. 94–96; Runia, *Doctrine,* pp. 18–56; Robert McAfee Brown, "Scripture and Tradition in the Theology of Karl Barth," *Scripture and Ecumenism,* pp. 26–28; Vawter, *Inspiration,* pp. 91–94; Barr, *Fundamentalism,* p. 214; and Rogers and McKim, *Authority,* p. 418.

5. K. Barth, *Church Dogmatics,* Vol. 1, pt. 2, 523, 529; Runia, *Doctrine,* pp. 57–80; and Rogers and McKim, *Authority,* pp. 423–424.

6. Smart, *Scripture,* p. 194; and Kelsey, *Scripture,* pp. 47–48.

provides us with a link to God and his self-disclosure in Jesus Christ. In the Scriptures we meet with an understanding of God, ourselves, our fellow humanity, the nature of the world, and life. In the text sinful people encounter a sovereign God who is present before them in an I-Thou relationship.[7]

Many other theologians appear to follow Barth in these understandings, either totally or in part.[8] Many theologians use a definition for the word of God which includes the concept of *viva vox*. Paradigms on the word of God often picture Jesus Christ as the word of God primarily, while the preaching and teaching office are a secondary manifestation, and the Scriptures are a tertiary expression. Theologians often speak of the authority of the Bible in terms of its ability to shape the identity of the Church and individual Christians. Numerous contemporaries of Barth were influenced by his description. Emil Brunner would use the same language, though he disagreed with Barth on issues such as natural revelation outside the biblical text. Likewise, Friedrich Gogarten would speak of two holy histories, one recorded in the text and the other in our own personal lives, and authority for us is established in the latter.[9] Perhaps the views of Oswald Loretz also belong here. He defines inerrancy of the Bible in terms of divine faithfulness, as does the language of the biblical authors (Hebrew *'emet* and Greek *aletheia*). Scriptures speak of a God of truth who will be faithful continually to his people to keep them from permanently straying from the truth. As with Barth this view moves behind the biblical text to affirm a God who deals personally with his people.[10]

Rudolf Bultmann offers us another significant existential mode for understanding the message and authority of the Bible. Bultmann declares the biblical message authoritative only when it confronts the individual in a situation to condemn inauthentic living and elicit the response—acceptance of freedom and a responsible life style. The source of this confrontation is the life and ethical imperative of Jesus, and the authority

---

7. Smart, *Scripture,* pp. 51–52; and Kelsey, *Scripture,* p. 47.

8. A. Jones, "Rendezvous," pp. 97–109, sees this as a model to which both Roman Catholics and Protestants can adhere.

9. Emil Brunner, *Revelation and Reason,* trans. Olive Wyon (Philadelphia: Westminster, 1946), pp. 3–430; Friedrich Gogarten, "Theology and History," trans. Louis de Grazia, *History and Hermeneutic,* pp. 35–81; and Richardson, "Biblical Scholarship," pp. 326–327.

10. Loretz, *Truth,* pp. 53–95, 114–156; and Vawter, *Inspiration,* pp. 150–153.

resides in the "existentiell" confrontation of the individual and not the "existential" interpretation of the text.[11] Bultmann was impressed by the thought of Martin Heidegger, and he used his philosophical categories to formulate theology in a new modern setting. Thus, the emphasis upon existence, being, and authenticity reflect a reigning philosophical world view of Bultmann's era.

Bultmann's strength was as an exegete. He was able to perceive the meaning of the biblical text, particularly in the New Testament, in the intellectual categories of that age. Impressed by how alien the New Testament thought milieu was compared to the modern way of thinking, Bultmann felt it necessary to express the message of the New Testament in forms that modern people could understand. Much of the "mythology" or symbolic way of speaking in the biblical era is simply not understood today. Therefore, the message had to be expressed in modern categories. For Bultmann the best form of modern discourse was the language of existence and encounter formulated by Martin Heidegger.[12]

The authoritative aspect of Scripture resided in those passages which proclaimed the Christ-event and produced a contemporary "revealing" and "saving" experience in the minds of the modern listeners. It is the task of the biblical historian not to discover the "real Jesus," as nineteenth century liberal Protestants had attempted. The biblical historian or theologian discovers those texts which express self-understanding of the ancient Christians and recovers them for modern expression to people in the Church today.[13]

For Barth, Bultmann, and others the authority of the Bible lies in its ability to encounter people in a deeply religious and intellectual fashion so as to change their lives. To describe authority in these terms is very subjective, yet it appears very practical.

The strength of this approach is that the living dynamism of the Bible is recaptured. The oral preaching of the ancient Church regains its authority in the worship and preaching of the modern Church. We are reminded of the need for preachers to proclaim a message to modern people from the context of the Bible. This position very honestly describes how

11. Bultmann, "General Truths and Christian Proclamation," trans. Schubert Ogden, *History and Hermeneutic*, pp. 153–162, and "Preaching: Genuine and Secularized," *Religion and Culture: Essays in Honor of Paul Tillich*, ed. Walter Leibrecht (New York: Harper and Row, 1959), pp. 236–242.

12. Bultmann, *Mythology*, pp. 35–85.

13. Kelsey, *Scripture*, p. 74, and "Protestant Attitudes," p. 157.

the text functions in the experiences of members in the community, or at least how it should function when the Bible is adequately preached.[14]

Dead Scholasticism and legalism of the book models of inspiration are avoided as well as the "dead historicism" of *Heilsgeschichte* models. Theologians are reminded to avoid the pitfall of bibliolatry and the creation of artificial concepts, and instead they are called to release the dynamic power of Scripture.[15]

Barth, in particular, provides a basis for viewing the canon as a unified whole. It is a source for preaching, and the word of God may come through it. This avoids the need for discriminating a core of writings, a theme, or an organizing principle, which then subordinates the rest of the canon.[16]

By placing the locus of authority in the modern existential situation the exegete is freed from the intellectual concepts of the ancient biblical world. This old world view may be demythologized in order to present the deeper meaning for modern people. Authority is placed into the hands of a living God who confronts his people.[17]

Criticisms may be leveled at the model, especially on the aspect of its subjectivity. Religious experience stands in the stead of the Bible as the source of authority, and philosophical presuppositions may qualify the understanding of that religious experience. In Bultmann's theology it is Heideggerian existentialism.[18] It is nineteenth and twentieth century liberal Protestantism revisited, and critics describe it as reductionistic in a different fashion. The reference to the *kergyma* or the existential encounter is similar to the essence or core of teachings sought in the "quest for the historical Jesus" which typified the nineteenth century theological endeavor.[19]

Existentialism may blur the distinction between the inspiration of

---

14. K. Barth, *The Word of God and the Word of Man,* trans. Douglas Horton (New York: Harper, 1957), pp. 9–327; and Kelsey, *Scripture,* p. 50.

15. Runia, *Doctrine,* pp. 160–161.

16. Kelsey, *Scripture,* p. 50.

17. Cunliffe-Jones. "A Congregationalist Contribution," *Symposium,* p. 45; Prenter, "Lutheran Contribution," pp. 98–100; and Hodgson, "God and the Bible," pp. 1–24.

18. Erich Dinkler, *Bibelauthorität und Bibelkritik,* Sammlung Gemeinverständlicher Vorträge und Schriften aus dem Gebeit der Theologie und Religionsgeschichte, Vol. 193 (Tübingen: Mohr, 1950), pp. 26–29; and W. Schweitzer, "Biblical Theology," pp. 146–147.

19. Richardson, *Science,* pp. 105–114.

God and the inward subjective feelings of the individual today. The feeling or emotional response of modern day listeners is highly elevated in importance. The call to authentic existence elicited by the text might move in as many different directions as there are listeners in the audience. The model calls upon people to respond to their feelings, and that might be dangerous. Why should an experience point beyond itself? Often it is an emotional response with no cognitive direction. A religious experience has no norm and is capable of diverse interpretation. The existential model may open Pandora's box.[20]

New theology may be constructed with little relationship to the text and the religious experiences recorded therein. The utilization of new philosophical models to contemporize the Christian message may cause it to move in radically new directions. The greater portion of the Christian tradition may be left behind.

Existential positions are dualistic in regard to the Scriptures, and this is most evident with Barth's model of the word of God. Scripture and the word of God become two separate realities. To call the Scriptures "fallible" and "human" separates them so much from God, it becomes difficult to see how God uses them.[21]

Existential positions, especially Bultmann's, do not take the historical dimension seriously. Bultmann uses extremely thorough textual work to obtain good insights into the New Testament; then he discards them for his modern existential theology under the rubric of demythologizing. This is due to the existential model which puts the message in personal and subjective categories. The concrete and the historical dimension are gone, and perhaps the desire to do careful scrutiny of the biblical text will be eroded eventually.[22]

Finally, many critics have pointed out that the myth and the message of the Scriptures cannot be separated easily.[23] The *kerygma* crouches deeply in the thought forms of ancient Hebrew and Greek thought; its extraction demands a new reconstruction with normative guidelines. To remove the "symbol" of the ancient world may strip away the message.

---

20. Dinkler, *Bibelauthorität*, pp. 29–33; Cunliffe-Jones, *Authority*, pp. 121, 133; Wright, "Modern World," pp. 223–224; and Pinnock, *Revelation*, pp. 167–168.
21. Runia, *Doctrine*, pp. 118–131.
22. Richardson, *Science*, p. 114.
23. W. Schweitzer, "Biblical Theology," pp. 146–147.

Maybe symbols are never really outdated and can still communicate meaning to their listeners.

The idea of retaining the symbols or the narrative dimension, because of its ability to communicate, has been advocated by some interpreters. They emphasize the importance of simple narrative in communication.

SYMBOLIC EXISTENTIALISM

A number of individuals are sensitive to literature and the nature of language. As they study the Bible it becomes evident that they are confronted with literature which cannot be reduced to simple logical, ideational, and positivistic categories. The material in the Old Testament especially demands a greater flexibility in treatment because of the diversity of literary forms. Biblical language is often poetic in form and mythic in origin, for such is the nature of literature.[24]

Scripture communicates a great deal to its readers and listeners in non-rational modes. Symbols communicate to the audience and frequently cause a response in emotional and artistic categories. These symbols often communicate meaning to the corporate Church in a way as to elicit a plethora of responses, all of which are valid. These responses include doctrine, liturgy, preaching, teaching, and art. As a result a number of theologians prefer to describe the communication of Scripture as a mode of symbolic and interpersonal communication.[25]

Revelation is the disclosure of the divine. God reveals himself not only in logical positivistic language, but in the fullest form of human expression. The Bible contains a wide range of diverse human expressions, all of which communicate meaning. Revelation is the disclosure of personal knowledge; often symbols communicate better than words, for language is often insufficient. (How often to we need an analogy to truly explain a rational argument?) Even Scripture is insufficient with its

24. Richardson, *Science*, pp. 142–163; Dulles, "The Theology of Revelation," *Theological Studies* 25 (1964): 43–58; Alonso-Schökel, *Word*, pp. 91–105; and Barr, *Scope*, pp. 1–17.

25. Dulles, "Revelation," pp. 43–58; Rene Latourelle, *Theology of Revelation* (Staten Island: Alba, 1966), pp. 9–508; Gabriel Moran, "The God of Revelation," *Commonweal* 85 (1967): 499–503; Alonso-Schökel, *Word*, pp. 296–299, 376–385; and Barr, *Scope*, pp. 1–17, 121–122.

language to state the fullness of revelation in Jesus Christ, so that the best communication of the divine love is often the visual symbols of the cross and empty tomb. (Perhaps the empty tomb emerged in the testimony of the Gospels with the seemingly more important resurrection appearances, because it was a graphic visual symbol!)[26]

Several authors have proposed such a model. Austin Farrar is mentioned by most writers as an early influence for the development of these ideas.[27] Farrar believed that inspiration did not create verbal propositions, but images by which truth could be expressed.[28] More recent advocates of this viewpoint include Gabriel Moran, Hans Frei, and Luis Alonso-Schökel, whose work, *The Inspired Word,* may be the fullest presentation of this understanding.[29]

According to the evaluation of David Kelsey several other significant theologians also engaged in this form of interpretation: Lionel Thornton, Paul Tillich, and Karl Barth. Thornton appears to construe the Bible as an album of symbols which seek to portray a divine cosmic process. Tillich, according to Kelsey, sees biblical symbols perform two roles: they describe the original revelatory event and they recreate a dependent revelatory event today. For him the Bible is a collection of expressions about the event in Jesus Christ, and they are our sole access to that original salvific event. Karl Barth is included because he sees a pattern of events in all of Scripture which parallel the actions of intent of Jesus' ministry. Barth appears to appeal to the biblical narratives as they are without critically reconstructing them. Scriptural narrative is authoritative because it occasions the possibility for a divine-human encounter, wherein the story "renders an agent" and recreates the original revelational event.[30] Kelsey's arguments are tremendously helpful for this study, but this author is cautious. Thorton would appear to fit the category of symbolic

26. Moran, *Scripture and Tradition* (New York: Herder, 1963), pp. 63–76, and *Theology of Revelation* (New York: Herder, 1966), pp. 217–231; and Dulles, "Revelation," pp. 43–58.

27. Farrar, *Glass,* passim, *A Rebirth of Images* (London: n.p., 1949), passim, *A Study in St. Mark* (London: n.p., 1951), passim, and *St. Matthew and St. Mark* (London: n.p., 1954), passim.

28. Richardson, *Science,* pp. 158–161.

29. Moran, *Scripture,* pp. 13–87, "What Is Revelation?" *Theological Studies* 25 (1964): 217–231, *Theology,* pp. 15–188, and "God," pp. 499–503; Alonso-Schökel, *Word,* pp. 19–385; and Hans Frei, *The Eclipse of Biblical Narrative: A Study in Eighteenth Century Hermeneutics* (New Haven: Yale, 1974), pp. 1–324.

30. Kelsey, *Scripture,* pp. 39–50, 57–83.

existentialism, but including Paul Tillich and Karl Barth may stretch the model.

This creative understanding has several advantages. Above all it recognizes the literary quality of the Bible. More than any other theory it accepts and works with the various literary forms found in the Bible. It honestly acknowledges the distinctive forms of expression and level of communication which can be rendered by various types of literature.

This model avoids some of the problems of earlier existential approaches. The content of the biblical text is not reduced to purely subjective existential categories. Not every text is seen in the context of human existence. Some are forms of art which appeal to the aesthetic sense. Some passages may not be expressively artistic, but they inspire a human response which leads to the creation of music, painting (especially during the Renaissance), sculpture, and literature. Previous existential theories do not seem to account for the impact the Bible has had upon the human psyche to produce art for two thousand years. This model really has a fuller psychological view of the total existential impact of the biblical text upon people.

This theory tends to see the wider function of the Bible in the Church. The impact of the Scriptures upon theology, teaching, catechesis, liturgy, Church art, and art forms in general is recognized. No other theory can be as far-reaching in its discussion about the impact of the biblical text.

Herein is the first of its weaknesses. The model can range so far that it no longer describes the authority of the Bible but rather its "impact." What is described includes the total artistic impact ("inspiration" in the artistic sense) of the Bible upon human culture. What results is a course in the humanities of the biblical tradition. A painter who does a biblical scene on a canvas is not affected by the authority of Scripture, for he or she does not necessarily have to be a believer; rather he or she is impressed with an image in the text. This model speaks not about the authority of the Bible, but its impression.

The model is amorphous. It seeks to include a wide concept of biblical communication or expression, and as a result the theory has not been given concrete expression by theological advocates. The mere fact that Kelsey may include other individuals, like Karl Barth, who fit other models in this book, implies the vague nature of this model. One could stretch this model enough to include almost every theologian who believes that the Bible communicates its message in vivid fashion. Perhaps

the model is truly a significant breakthrough in the discussion of authority, but it needs to be developed more.

Finally, the model could very easily fall into the pitfalls faced by
the other theories. Perhaps, if developed, this model could begin to speak
of the plenary inspiration of images rather than words. The vague nature
of its understanding not only allows it to escape criticism aimed at other
models, but also makes it able to develop their same deficiencies.[31]

COMMON EXISTENTIALISM

Despite the criticisms which may be directed at existential theories,
they appear to be the most popular mode of understanding biblical authority. This can be said only when one admits that many preachers and
teachers use the existential model without necessarily realizing it. What
they apply to their understanding of the biblical text is a more common,
everyday form of existential appropriation.

A less radical mode of existential interpretation sees the biblical text
as authoritative when it describes and speaks to situations parallel to our
own. The human condition changes little in the endless millennia; the
dilemmas of those people remind us of our own. Their elicited response
may be a guideline for our response once the continuity is understood.
The text tells what the faith once was, so that we may ascertain what it
should be now.[32] We do not transfer biblical habits naively to our age,
such as the wearing of hats in Corinth, but we seek to understand the
rationale behind the message. If it is applicable, we apply it, though the
form be different and the results be the opposite of what once was. This
method seeks the spirit not the letter of meaning in the text. Gerhard von
Rad declared that the best preaching was that which authentically repeats
the textual account and relives the experience.[33] Therein we find our common human bond with ancient spiritual forebears as we encounter the
same God.

The text may speak a strikingly clear message to the modern situa-

31. John Ballie, *The Idea of Revelation in Recent Thought* (Oxford: University
Press, 1956), p. 38; and Richardson, *Science*, p. 162.

32. Bright, *Authority*, p. 30.

33. Von Rad, *God at Work in Israel*, trans. John Marks (Nashville: Abingdon,
1980), pp. 9–18.

tion. The preacher may repeat the biblical message to the congregation as though they were the original audience. Sometimes the dramatic re-creation of the original setting may captivate the imagination of the lis-teners. Nor is it scandalous (contrary to Bultmann) to repeat the myth of images of the bygone age, for myth and symbol speak a more universal message than mere history or science. We never outgrow the power of mythic images. Myth must point to the transcendent reality and never be pawned off as mere scientific empirical reality or propositional revela-tion. Many ancient myths may not correspond to modern scientific real-ity, but they still communicate effectively to the human mind. Biblical symbols or myths have become such a part of Western culture that they still communicate at least some message to the audience. When the human situation parallels that of the text, the symbols in the text may speak with authority.

This position affirms the centrality of preaching and teaching. It en-ables the listener to avoid difficulties in the text, such as an outmoded world view, because it no longer speaks to our situation. The preacher merely omits what no longer communicates sensibly. What speaks to our situation is then authoritative. Preachers are able to make the Bible rel-evant for their people, and frequently they awaken a new interest in the text which leads to an increase in the authority of the Bible in the lives of the people.

However, the preacher can be very selective in drawing upon texts for the sermons, so that material incompatible with his or her opinions are deleted under the pretext of being irrelevant today. This is the greatest weakness of this model. The biblical text speaks without authority when it has been winnowed. Perhaps what is omitted because of its apparent ancient obscurity was really the important key to unlocking the meaning of the entire text. (If so, Bultmann may be correct in his assumption that the core message is lost in the mythology.) The entire process may de-generate into interesting renditions of Bible stories, and a trite Sunday School experience alone will remain.

Another problem is to determine the degree of similarity in life sit-uations. Our modern way of thinking and living is often different from that of our biblical counterparts. How much similarity must there be be-fore a comparison is legitimate? How much difference do we tolerate as we apply their experience to our own? The preacher must make this decision subjectively while running the risk of trying to make people think like ancient Hebrews.[34] This hermeneutical process is acceptable only if another norm is used to determine the applicability of the texts, and this will be the locus of authority, not the existential situation. This theory actually faces many of the same problems encountered by the critical European theologians with their models.

CONCLUSION

In conclusion existential models are the most dynamic and appealing, but they are the most subjective, for they run the risk of leading preaching into theological dead ends and obscure trivialities. Preachers are perhaps the people most attracted to this model, and they are the ones who most readily fall into the traps.

34. Barr, *Bible*, pp. 47–49.

Chapter Eleven

CHRISTOCENTRIC MODELS

A selected norm taken from part of the biblical text or a crucial theological concept may serve as a *norma normans* to interpret the rest of the Bible. This authority within the Bible may direct the exegete in interpreting the various texts.

Christians usually appeal to the centrality of Christ or the proclamation of the Gospel as such a norm, though only few interpreters are consistent in using this principle in their methodology. Certainly most Christian interpreters see the person and message of Christ as the most important part of the biblical message. Most would claim that this is the chief hermeneutical principle and criterion of ultimate authority. However, in reality most interpreters are actually guided by other principles when it comes to their treatment of the biblical material.[1]

Martin Luther is singled out frequently as exemplar of this method, for he could call the Bible the cradle wherein laid the Christ child. The formula *solus Christus* ("Christ alone") was the undergirding formula behind the most well known Reformation formulas *sola gratia* ("grace alone"), *sola fide* ("faith alone"), and *sola scriptura* ("Scripture alone"). The Christological principle was prior to the Scripture principle. The dicta *was Christum treibt* and *die Christum predigen und treiben*

---

1. John Marsh, "History and Interpretation," *Symposium,* pp. 181–197; Cunliffe-Jones, *Authority,* p. 119, and "Congregationalist Contribution," p. 46; Earl Palmer, "The Pastor as a Biblical Christian," *Biblical Authority,* p. 128; and Smart, *Scripture,* pp. 197–215.

("what preaches Christ and drives him home") could lead Luther to higher critical conclusions about the text. His desire to exclude James and Esther from the canon for their lack of Gospel proclamation and his willingness to condemn as false the passage in James 2:24 ("a man is justified by works") betray the elevation of a Christological principle over any inspiration model in the modern sense. His critical methodology may have laid the foundations for modern *Heilsgeschichte* and existential models.[2]

Karl Barth is a good modern example, for he uses the Christological principle as the norm for his concept of the existential encounter. Since the Bible points to Christ as the significant salvific event, Christ is the locus of authority who brings salvation in the preached encounter. Christ is the *logos theou* "originally and immediately," while the written canon is the word of God only "derivately and mediately" as it testifies to Him. The *viva vox* and living tradition of the Church depend on Christ for authority. Tradition should be governed and normed by Scripture, but it should not be ignored, as some Protestants have done.[3] Barth's position is paralleled by Peter Taylor Forsyth, Friedrich Gogarten, Hubert Cunliffe-Jones, John Reid, Charles Dodd, and George Tavard.[4]

There are three different ways to view Christ as the center of this process. One might emphasize Christ as event; hence the death and resurrection would constitute the Gospel *kerygma* and the chief locus of authority. Luther's emphasis on the justification principle would typify this approach. By interpreting the various texts of Scripture the theologian would seek to emphasize the divine love and the forgiveness of sins in the event of Jesus' death and resurrection. Often a typological approach

---

2. Paul Althaus, *The Theology of Martin Luther*, trans. Robert Schultz (Philadelphia: Fortress, 1966), pp. 72–102; Werner Elert, *The Structure of Lutheranism*, trans. Walter Hanson (St. Louis: Concordia, 1962), pp. 179–191; Bengt Hagglund, *History of Theology*, trans. Gene Lund (St. Louis: Concordia, 1968), pp. 220–223; and Rogers and McKim, *Authority*, pp. 75–88.

3. K. Barth, *Church Dogmatics*, Vol. 1, pt. 1, 47–292, and Vol. 1, pt. 2, 457–740; M. Barth, *Conversation with the Bible* (New York: Holt, Rinehart & Winston, 1964), pp. 173–197; Bryant, *Authority*, pp. 91–94; Richardson, "Biblical Scholarship," pp. 321–322; Reid, *Authority*, pp. 194–221, who notes that Karl Barth could be critical of Calvin for being too close to an inspirationist view; and Barr, *Bible*, p. 19.

4. Gogarten, "Theologie," pp. 390–394; Dodd, *Authority*, pp. 216–219; Cunliffe-Jones, *Authority*, pp. 19, 119, 133; Reid, *Authority*, pp. 236–245, 269–279; and Bryant, *Authority*, pp. 29, 85–90.

to the Old Testament would seek to identify parallels or predictions in the text which point toward the Christ event in the New Testament. This was typical of the Reformation theology.

A more modern approach seeks to critically evaluate the biblical text in its historical setting in order to more clearly understand the mission of Christ. Such an approach tends to emphasize the person and teachings of Jesus more than the passion; the death and resurrection event as an act which brings forgiveness is de-emphasized in relation to the message and moral imperatives of Jesus. Nineteenth century liberal Protestant scholarship, which tended to disregard the dogmas of traditional orthodoxy, sought to rediscover the teachings and saying of the "historical Jesus." Lives of Jesus were written by Friedrich Schleiermacher, Ernst Renan, Ferdinand Baur, and others who sought to strip away the accretions added by the Gospel writers to discover the earliest traditions and more adequately perceive the person called Jesus of Nazareth. The belief in the death and resurrection of Jesus as a saving event was understood to be a primitive belief; only Jesus' moral vision had true lasting relevance for the modern era. Protestant theologians of the late nineteenth century, like Albrecht Ritschl, Adolph von Harnack, and Ernst Troelsch, tried to construct a modern theology upon the results of these investigations. They summarized the teachings of Jesus to be an affirmation of the "Fatherhood of God and the Brotherhood of Man," a mandate for the universal ethical and social mission of the modern Church. This understanding conformed more to the values of nineteenth century German idealism than to the biblical text. But it was an attempt to understand Christ as a central principle in the Scriptures and his teachings as the central authority.[5]

Twentieth century theologians who are heir to this tradition neither are as optimistic about finding the essential core or the historical Jesus, nor are as reductionistic in their methodology. After the work of Martin Kähler, Johannes Weiss, and Albert Schweitzer the quest for the histor-

---

5. Albrecht Ritschl, "Instruction in the Christian Religion," *Three Essays,* trans. Philip Hefner (Philadelphia: Fortress, 1972), pp. 221–291; Adolph von Harnack, *What Is Christianity?* trans. Thomas Bailey Saunder (New York: Harper and Row, 1957), pp. 10–301; Ernst Troelsch, *The Social Teachings of the Christian Churches,* 2 vols., trans. Olive Wyon (Chicago: University Press, 1960), 2:461–1013; and Walter Rauschenbusch, *A Theology for the Social Gospel* (Nashville: Abingdon, 1945), pp. 1–279.

ical Jesus was surrendered.[6] Scholars realized that the Gospels were very subjective documents, confessions of faith in the thought milieu of the ancient world, and they were impenetrable to the eyes of modern critical historiography. All we had were the confessions of faith of the ancient Church; we could never be sure of the nature of the historical Jesus, and we would have to content ourselves with an approximate understanding of his original message. The theological response to this was to accept the subjective confession of faith by the ancient Church and affirm the Christ of faith rather than the Jesus of history. Most twentieth century theologians would view the Christ of faith, the living Lord of the Church, as the source of authority. This is the starting point for many existential models of authority which declare the present encounter with Christ as the authoritative experience.[7]

Christological models have the primary strength of emphasizing the heart of the Christian faith, be it the Gospel *kerygma* or Christ's salvific activity, the teachings of Jesus, or the present Lordship of Christ. Critical scholarly insight is accepted even to the point of declaring some biblical material to be inferior when it seems to contradict or obscure the clarity of the Gospel. The dynamic of the preached word is understood as the model to explain the relationship between Christ, canon, and tradition. The whole structure revolves organically around the center point of the faith, and this promotes better theological balance. The human and the divine aspects of the text may be seen, for a particular text may be viewed in critical fashion while permitting divine encounter for the reader. The conservative and liberal extremes of ascribing authority to the very words or ignoring the message of the text are avoided. Instead, the unity of the Bible manifests itself in the person of Christ. The Bible is inspired not in itself but through Jesus Christ, and it becomes the Word of God through Jesus Christ.[8]

---

6. Martin Kähler, *The So-Called Historical Jesus and the Historic, Biblical Christ,* trans. Carl Braaten (Philadelphia: Fortress, 1964), pp. 42–148; Johannes Weiss, *Jesus' Proclamation of the Kingdom of God,* trans. Richard Hyde Hiers and David Larrimore Holland (Philadelphia: Fortress, 1971), pp. 57–136; and Albert Schweitzer, *The Quest for the Historical Jesus,* trans. W. Montgomery (New York: Macmillan, 1968), pp. 1–402.

7. Barnabas Nagy, "A Reformed Contribution," trans. Dorothy Barton *Symposium,* p. 84.

8. Cunliffe-Jones, *Authority,* pp. 13, 41, 119, 133; and W. Schweitzer, "Biblical Theology," pp. 147–149.

However, weaknesses slowly surface. An exegete may easily subordinate part of the biblical text for the sake of another. He or she may overturn an established ethical norm by declaring it inferior or irrevelant to the Gospel. Those texts which make the preacher uncomfortable may be ignored on a particular issue. Interpretations of certain passages may be distorted by undue Christological emphasis which finds Christ in every passage, until the text can no longer speak a particular word of its own.[9] Finally, the experience of the living Christ can become a subjective experience of the believer, an inspirational feeling with no objective norm to control or guide it. The word of God may be separated from the text and located in human experience.[10]

CANON WITHIN A CANON

Within this context an interesting debate has arisen in the modern era. Throughout the history of interpretation it is evident that Christians tended to use and quote certain portions of the biblical text more than others. Modern theologians have begun to describe this tendency in a more formal way by devising a hermeneutical principle to describe and legitimate the choice of certain biblical texts.

Ernst Käsemann's work enters into the discussion at this point. He believes that the Gospel, or the principle of justification by faith through grace as articulated by Paul, is not only the interpretative norm, it creates a "canon within the canon." Works like Romans, Galatians, and 1 and 2 Corinthians convey the Gospel in its purest form, and therefore they are more authoritative than other parts of Scripture. Divergent views and theological strains in the rest of Scripture must be subordinate to these works. Hence, the *frühkatholismus* ("early catholic") tendencies of the pastorals and later New Testament epistles with their views of episcopacy, creedalism, formalized worship, institutionalization, and restraint are inferior to the radical charismatic and egalitarian theology of Paul's

---

9. Wilhelm Vischer, *The Witness of the Old Testament to Christ*, 2 vols. (London: Lutterworth, 1949), 1:7–256, represents such a work which seeks to analyze the Old Testament in radical Christological categories.

10. Pinnock, "Three Views," p. 59.

early letters.[11] This theology is the norm for the rest of Scripture, Scripture is the norm for developing Christian tradition, and tradition is the norm for Church life and practice. At times in Church history the Gospel norm must be used to correct and reform traditions just as it corrects later New Testament theology. Käsemann's views attract many.[12]

The strengths of this view are several. Christ is affirmed as the center of the faith, and in particular the Gospel proclamation. Diverse theologies are recognized in the canon, and a way of integrating them is offered that does not compromise critical scholarship. In fact, critical attempts to highlight differences are affirmed. Furthermore all theologians consciously or unconsciously draw upon a select core of biblical texts for their theology, and frequently Romans, Galatians, and 1 and 2 Corinthians provide the bulk of the material. Käsemann boldly proclaims in his method what other theologians do quietly in practice, and such bold admission avoids self-delusion and possible misdirection. Finally, this view is a clear manifesto for continuing reform in the Church—the Gospel is the axe by which the dead roots are pruned—*ecclesia reformanda est* ("the Church must be reformed continually").

Weaknesses are as follows: It has the taint of Marcionism. Elevating a few books in such precise and clear fashion is an invitation to exclude other works gradually from the canon or the theological endeavor. These other works, especially the Old Testament, may exhibit a normative function by correcting, clarifying, and laying the foundation for thought in the more significant theological segments.[13] Pauline epistles may be important, but their isolation in the theological task invites disaster by destroying the unity of the whole and the beautiful symphonic harmony of the divergent theological traditions. (This diversity is praised in those very same Pauline letters!)

---

11. Ernst Käsemann, "Is the Gospel Objective?" pp. 48–62, "Ministry and Community in the New Testament," pp. 63–94, "The Canon of the New Testament and the Unity of the Church," pp. 95–107, and "An Apologia for Primitive Christian Eschatology," pp. 169–195, *Essays on New Testament Themes,* trans. William John Montague, Studies in Biblical Theology, Vol. 41 (London: SCM, 1964), pp. 48–107, 169–195, and "Paul and Early Catholicism," pp. 236–251, and "Unity and Multiplicity in the New Testament Doctrine of the Church," pp. 252–259, *New Testament Questions of Today,* trans. Montague and Wilfrid Bunge (Philadelphia: Fortress, 1969), pp. 236–259.

12. Werner Georg Kümmel, "Notwendigkeit und die Grenze des neutestamentliche Kanons," *Zeitschrift für Theologie und Kirche* 47 (1950): 277–313.

13. Barr, *Bible,* pp. 160–162.

The method has the smell of denominationalism. Käsemann uses the classic Lutheran formulation of the justification principle to exclude the early institutionalization of primitive Christianity, and Hans Küng is his chief critic to show how this excludes Roman Catholic emphases from the canon. Undue emphasis upon one theological aspect, no matter how important it may be, hurts the great ecumenicity of the modern Church. Käsemann's *sola scriptura* principle has become *sola pars ecclesiae*.[14] Käsemann has the Protestant penchant for finding unity in the canon by selecting a theme like justification to organize the text.[15]

A methodological procedure like this sacrifices the unity of diverse themes in the canon. Choosing one theme as exclusive to the others is sectarian at best and heretical at worst. Precedents are set which could lead into theological tangents and dead ends.[16] Faithful exegesis must strive to see the message of the text in light of the greater canonical tradition according to modern biblical critics.[17]

Finally, the method is too subjective. The exegete may exclude theological tendencies with which he or she does not concur, so that a word of judgment might be missed, new insights lost, and the impetus for reform removed, and these were the original goals of Käsemann's work.[18]

As is the case with other Christological models this particular approach sounds eminently appropriate for handling the text in a Christian perspective. Many Christians would find themselves in agreement with the basic presuppositions which Käsemann advances. But in actual practice several problems arise which can become the undoing of this hermeneutical process.

---

14. Hans Küng, " 'Early Catholicism' in the New Testament as a Problem in Controversial Theology," *The Council in Action,* trans. Cecil Hastings (New York: Sheed and Ward, 1963), pp. 168–176; John Elliot, "The New Testament Is Catholic: A Re-evaluation of Sola Scriptura," *Una Sancta* 23 (1966): 3–19; Kelsey, *Scripture,* p. 118; and Bartlett, *Shape,* p. 136.

15. Kelsey, *Scripture,* p. 118.

16. Willi Marxsen, *Der Frünkatholizimus in Neuen Testament* (Neukirchen: Moers, 1958), p. 59; Karl Schelke, *Die Petrusbriefe,* Herders Theologische Kommentar zum Neuen Testament, Vol. 12, pt. 2 (Basle: Herder, 1961), p. 245; and Hans von Campenhausen, "Das Problem der Ordnung im Urchristentum und in der Alten Kirche," *Tradition und Leben* (Tübingen; Mohr, 1962), p. 162.

17. Childs, *Theology,* pp. 91–219; and Bartlett, *Shape,* pp. 137–146.

18. Küng, *Structures of the Church* (South Bend: Notre Dame, 1968), pp. 145–147.

Conclusion

Christological models are affirmed by everyone in theory, for they encapsulate the most important part of the Christian faith and emphasize the centrality of the Christ event in some form. In actuality only a few exegetes and theologians apply a consistent Christological model. In practice there is great subjectivity on the part of the exegete. How one interprets Christ or the Gospel will have great implications for the hermeneutical procedure, and this interpretation may not be articulated easily, nor will consensus be readily established among the theologians who seek to use such a model.

Chapter Twelve

MODELS OF LIMITATION

A different approach to understanding the authority of the Bible is to limit that authority and declare that the Bible should not be used in such predominant fashion for the creation of theology as advocates of other positions might affirm. This category includes a wide range of attitudes. Some individuals believe that the canon should never have been closed; rather we should have continued to work with Scriptures (writings in the plural) rather than a Scripture or canon. Other theologians recognize the legitimacy of the canon; they simply wish to limit its authority. Roman Catholic minimalists often sought to limit the authority of the Scripture so as to elevate the authority of the Church. Liberal Protestant theologians in the modern era have spoken of the Bible as one among many inspired works, or as an authoritative source of theology along with other sources.

OPEN CANON

A common viewpoint advocates an open canon, which would declare the canonization process of the fourth century a mistake or failure of nerve.[1] The Scriptures have a religious authority in the way they were viewed prior to the fourth century, but there would be no normative canon or Bible. Two different arguments might be advanced. The first attributes all authority to Christ, and since his is a living authority, crystallization of authority in a fixed, written book is counterproductive. Writings which testify clearly to Christ should be received and used, but no limit would be placed on which particular documents are to the thus received. The

---

1. Nineham, "The Use of the Bible in Modern Theology," *Bulletin of the John Rylands Library* 52 (1969): 198; and Barr, *Bible*, pp. 43–44.

ongoing spiritual life of the Church would determine which books ought to be added.

A second viewpoint might begin with the presupposition of progressive revelation, a point of view advocated by many of the preceding theologians. This progressive revelation may be seen as still operative today in the movement of the Holy Spirit to actualize the message and work of Christ in the world. Since spiritual growth never ceases, it would be wrong to fix it in one book which reflects only a stage in the development of the Christian tradition.

Advocates of an open canon often arrive at their position after the study of canon history both in the Old Testament's development in Israel and in the New Testament's development in the ancient Church (see below). They perceive that a canonization process occurs when the believing community finds itself or its faith threatened by outside forces. The growth of the canon was always the quest for theological authority. A corpus of literature would be created out of normative religious writings to serve as a model for the faith, a source for belief and practice. Each generation actually played a role leading up to a grand period in history when specific canons were created, for each generation sought to contemporize the message of the faith for its era. Those people who actually created a canon were performing an ultimate act of contemporizing the message. They engaged in a legitimate search for unity of the faith in the face of social-religious change. Unfortunately, when a literary canon is created, the rather fluid process of reinterpreting the traditions anew for each generation can be frozen into a static or rigid form.[2]

Theologians need to be aware of the history of the canon and the social-religious causes behind the canonization process. In this way they become more sensitive to the fluid and dynamic nature of the canonization process, and they are less likely to treat the Scripture as a fixed and rigid entity. They will be more true to the tradition developing process which lies behind Scripture and they will more faithfully engage in the contemporary theologizing process. The canon provides a classic model for the presentation of traditions, but does not function as the exclusive model. No stage is more authoritative, for the people of God must continue to

---

2. Robert Laurin, ''Tradition and Canon,'' *Tradition and Theology in the Old Testament,* ed. Douglas Knight (Philadelphia: Fortress, 1977), pp. 261–274.

engage in a canonizing process by ever hearing the Spirit anew.[3] Robert Laurin says it well:

> For tradition history demonstrates the fundamental point that the development of canon was a legitimate search for authority by the community, but the final canonization was an illegitimate closure of that process by the community at one point in history.[4]

The advocates of an open canon certainly sense the vibrancy of development in the theology of the Church. They recognize how religious traditions grow to meet new challenges and situations. The word of God may be perceived as living reality in the *viva vox* more than in other models. The idyllic status of the pre-fourth century Church is sought, wherein no canon existed and the Spirit's activity was sensed in many writings. Finally, provision would be made for recognizing deeply insightful spiritual works produced throughout the Christian tradition.

However, the position runs great risks. Without an objective norm for doing theology the possibility of new sectarian movements and new theological ideas looms large. Irresponsible rather than responsible ideas may blossom and flourish. Belief systems may develop which become wildly eschatological, for such has often been the case with the popular religion of the people which also ignores objective norms. Millennial beliefs and ideas such as the rapture (a concept created by a prophetess in Scotland during the 1830's) would emerge in the mainline Church as they now do in fringe groups.[5] Without the apostolic witness as the norm, which at least has the benefit of historical proximity to the founder and the founding event (Jesus and the resurrection), the Church will lack a norm by which to gauge new theological ideas.

LIMITED AUTHORITY

Various theologians have sought to limit the authority of the Bible because they wish to elevate other "authorities" to equal or greater status.

---

3. Ibid.
4. Ibid., p. 261.
5. Dave McPherson, *The Incredible Cover-Up: The True Story of the Pre-Trib Rapture* (Plainfield, New Jersey: Logos International, 1975), passim.

This tendency may be found among both Roman Catholic and Protestants.

A number of Roman Catholic theologians in the pre-modern era sought to minimalize the authority of the Scriptures as a way of critically responding to Protestant theologians with their strong emphasis upon *sola scriptura*. Leonhard Less or Lessius (1586) initiated many of these arguments by implying that inspiration was merely a negative assistance to avoid error, and the books become truly Sacred Scripture by virtue of a later approval by the Holy Spirit and the Church.[6] Later Roman Catholics who affirmed the idea of negative assistance included Francisco Suarez (1599–1628), Jacques Bonfrere (1625), Richard Simon (1680), Vincent Contenson (1681), Johann Jahn (1802), Jan Herman Janssens (1818), and Franz Heinrich Reusch (1870).[7] Other theologians emphasized the subsequent approval of the books by the testimony of either the Holy Spirit or the Church. Advocates included Jacques Bonfrere (1625), Sixtus of Siena (1575), and Daniel Bonifacius Haneberg (1850).[8]

These views were disowned subsequently by the Roman Catholic Church. Vatican I condemned especially the views of Jahn (''negative assistance'') and Haneberg (''subsequent approval''). Weaknesses with their theories were perceived correctly. If Scripture has merely negative assistance or ecclesiastical approval, it does not really differ from official Church statements by individuals or councils. That denies the authority of the Bible too radically, and blurs the distinction between Scripture and tradition. If negative assistance from error betokens Scripture, could not any book which is error-free be said to have been inspired by God? Scripture is the same as any literature. These theories not only limited Scripture's authority, they deprived it of any unique character whatever.[9]

---

6. Burtchaell, *Catholic Theories*, pp. 44–52; and Vawter, *Inspiration*, pp. 63–65.

7. Jacques Bonfrere, *In Totam Scripturam Sacram Praeloquia* (n.p.: 1625), passim; Richard Simon, *Histoire critique de vieux Testament* (Paris: n.p., 1680), passim; Vincent Contenson, *Theologia Mentis et Cordis* (Lugduni: Arnaud, 1681), passim; Johann Jahn, *Einleitung in den göttlichen Bücher des Alten Bundes*, 2nd ed. (Vienna: Wappler and Back, 1802), passim; Jan Herman Janssens, *Hermenutica Sacra* (n.p.: 1818), passim; and Franz Heinrich Reusch, *Lehrbuch der Einleitung in das Alte Testament*, 4th ed. (Freiburg: Herder, 1870), passim, and *Bibel und Natur*, 4th ed. (Bonn: Weber, 1876), passim. The work of these individuals is evaluated by Burtchaell, *Catholic Theories*, pp. 44–52; and Vawter, *Inspiration*, pp. 63–68.

8. Daniel Bonifacius Haneberg, *Versuch einer Geschichte der biblischen Offenbarung* (n.p.: 1850), passim. The views of these individuals are evaluated by Vawter, *Inspiration*, pp. 67–70.

9. Burtchaell, *Catholic Theories*, p. 52.

Protestant theologians influenced by Romanticism also sought to limit the authority of the Bible. Friedrich Ernst Schleiermacher is the classic theologian who introduced the dimension of human experience and feeling into the formulation of theology. He believed that these books were inspired because they best communicated the spirit of Christ. The *gemeingeist* ("community spirit") of the ancient Church produced them. But this spirit of Christ need not be limited to just the works of the canon, nor did revelation need to be limited to just the Bible. Other romantic thinkers believed that the inspiration in the biblical text was equal to that found in other religious literature. This opinion was voiced by Johann Gottfried Herder (1744–1803), Joannes David Michaelis, Johann Jakob Griesbach, and others in the nineteenth century as well as in more recent times.[10]

The developing critical methodologies of the nineteenth and twentieth centuries further encouraged this speculation. Other theologians pointed out the cultural and historical fixity of certain biblical expressions and modes of thought, and they advocated seeking those absolute categories to which the biblical images point in a new language mode. Theology would be best formulated by recourse to eternal ideas rather than by slavish bondage to worn biblical expressions and the authority of the biblical text. Men like Adolph von Harnack typified the nineteenth century quest for the historical Jesus and the quintessence of Hebrew thought, for therein the deeper ethical meaning was hidden behind the temporal forms.[11] In similar fashion twentieth century theologians like Harry Emerson Fosdick sought the "abiding experiences" of eternal life, the Kingdom of God, and the presence of the Spirit behind changing biblical categories.[12] But all of these theologians were calling for the limitation of the Bible's authority in either direct or indirect fashion as one tried to discern and elevate the grand ideals toward which the Bible pointed.

Considerations of the intellectual thought forms in relation to the social milieu found in the Bible has further encouraged these theologians. Modern scholarship has revealed the diversity of thought and even contradiction at times found in biblical tradition. The mere presence of such

---

10. Friedrich Ernst Schleiermacher, *The Christian Faith,* 2 vols., ed. Hugh Ross MacKintosh and James Stewart (New York: Harper and Row, 1963), 2:591–619; Richardson, *Science,* pp. 78–84; and Vawter, *Inspiration,* pp. 89–90.

11. Harnack, *Christianity,* pp. 72–74 et passim; and Reid, *Authority,* p. 179.

12. Fosdick, *Modern Use,* pp. 103, 129, et passim; and Bryant, *Authority,* p. 117.

diverse theological traditions seems to demand a limitation of biblical authority according to some scholars.[13] Other theologians approach the argument from the perspective of the social-historical conditioning of certain ways of thinking. If the extensive use of the Bible for theology demands a return to biblical modes of thought and an essential denial of our modern way of thinking, then limitation of the biblical authority for theology is necessary. Otherwise, we must brainwash our modern churchgoers to think like ancient people in order to understand the text.[14] Often the recourse of these theologians is to some existential model for interpretation (Rudolf Bultmann is the classic example).

Finally, a number of theologians seek to limit Scripture usage in theology by clarifying which sources should be used in the theological endeavor. Any theological work uses not only Scripture but hidden presuppositions of the author's world view. Every theology uses a philosophical model, be it Plato, Aristotle, common sense philosophy, Romanticism, process philosophy, or any other system. No theologian works without intellectual and cultural presuppositions. Honesty would demand a clear articulation of what those different sources are. The Bible is an authoritative norm only in conjunction with other norms, and such norms are said to include the *regulum fidei* ("rule of the faith"), the present status of the human arts and sciences, human emotional needs, and concrete existential situations. A good theologian must first be aware of the sources, then organize and relate them in balanced theological foundations. Otherwise the hidden presuppositions will arise and devour the entire theology. Phenomenological theologians are particularly concerned with groundsweeping so as to begin reconstruction of theology in balanced fashion on these norms.[15]

All of these critical thinkers appreciate the wider range of human experience, and they recognize the human intellectual development for a renewed proclamation of the Christian message. They are aware of the intellectual and cultural context of the Bible and the limitations of thought forms which originated in that era. Though their methods are subjective, discipline is brought into the methodology by recourse to the philosoph-

13. John Knox, *The Early Church and the Coming Great Church* (Nashville: Abingdon, 1955), pp. 11–155; and *The Church and the Reality of Christ* (New York: Harper and Row, 1962), pp. 119–147.

14. Barr, *Bible*, pp. 89–111.

15. Edward Farley, *Ecclesial Man: A Social Phenomenology of Faith and Reality* (Philadelphia: Fortress, 1975), pp. 3–272.

ical and empirical sciences. A mature and self-critical approach is taken to the evaluation of the text and the formulation of theology. A message which is intellectually compatible with modern human knowledge is the ultimate goal.

But therein is the danger. Which reigning *Weltanschauung* will offer itself to be the handmaid of theology? The philosophical assumptions of Schleiermacher, Harnack, Bultmann, and Farley are all different. One senses the differences between the throbbing pulse of early German Romanticism, later German positivistic idealism, and modern scientific empiricism underlying the different theological offerings. Each theologian would move in a different theological direction, and the Church would be left with neither identity nor continuity. How does one determine which outside factors are to be considered equal to the biblical authority, and where do theologians draw the line? The possibility looms that our theology will melt into mere subjectivity, emotional feelings, pious longings, and philosophical meanderings for a limited audience that may quickly be dated.

Models which seek to limit the authority of the Bible in relationship to other norms face a problem. What should those other norms be? A theology could quickly move into one direction and become a sectarian dead end. One may sweep a demon out of the front door while another sneaks in the back door.

Chapter Thirteen

HISTORICAL EMERGENCE OF THE AUTHORITATIVE BIBLE

The preceding survey of opinions concerning the locus of biblical authority reveals the complexity of issues involved in this quest. The proliferation of these opinions is a characteristic of the last two centuries of theological reflection, an age of critical self-examination by Christian thinkers in the face of changing scientific and social worldviews. Thus the majority of viewpoints considered in this book have been expressed by theologians in the past two centuries.

Increased sensitivity to the complexity of these issues has arisen, in part, due to the modern interest in biblical studies. Modern scholarship of the last two centuries has revealed thought forms alien to our own in the biblical text. We had too often read the Bible in a naive and uncritical fashion, which meant we merely read our own cultural and religious values into the text. But modern scholarship has forced us to read the text more honestly in an effort to perceive what it said in its own social-historical context. Though articles of the faith were not overturned, the nuances of our articulations were changed to more accurately reflect the message of the text.

A more faithful understanding of the message found in the biblical text has affected us deeply. Theologians have been led to transcend the narrow articulations of their own denominations. We have realized that the diversity which lay in the biblical traditions was really the source of some modern diversity among denominations. In reality, no one Church body could lay claim to the true position; rather different faith stances were rooted authentically in the biblical traditions. Then again, some of the modern distinctions which divided Christians were seen to be artificial creations of the medieval and early modern periods. We were making finer distinctions in our theology than were to be found in the biblical tradition. Instead, the Bible manifested a diverse range of religious expressions. This diversity in the text testified to the plurality found in the apostolic Church. Their diversity was seen to be greater than the differences between mainline denominations today, and yet they could view themselves as the unified body of Christ. This insight declared to us that unity in the Church today is not confounded by diversity but perhaps may be strengthened by it. Thus the greatest contribution of modern biblical studies to Christians today may be the impetus for ecumenical relationships.

Modern scholarship provides not only contributions to understanding the meaning of biblical texts but also insight into how the biblical text arose. Discussion of the nature of biblical authority may be enhanced by the consideration of such insights. Understanding the developmental process behind the canon may not answer the question concerning authority, but it may help us clarify and qualify some of the models previously discussed.

ORIGIN OF BIBLICAL LITERATURE

Biblical literature arose first in oral form as stories, poems, legends, epics, myths, hymns, and sayings. This literature reflected the feelings of the people and came from various settings in everyday life. The unifying factor which brought much of the oral literature together was a faith expression of people testifying to the goodness and grace of God on their behalf. People of Israel recalled Yahweh's gracious actions in the exodus (salvation history material of the Pentateuch and the prophets) and in the created order of the world (wisdom and psalms). Ancient Christians recalled the sayings, signs, and passion of Jesus in similar fashion, though the oral trajectories continued only for a generation instead of centuries, as in the Old Testament. Oral material was brought together in cycles, precipitated into written form, and was woven together to become the biblical text.

Thus the text was created in the community of faith, be it Israel or the ancient Church, over a gradual period of time. Key experiences were perceived and interpreted by eyes of faith which sought to give expression to the meaning of those events for others in the community. The interpretation may have been done by an individual, such as a bard, poet, prophet, sage, or apostle. Or the interpretation may have been developed slowly among the group itself from which an individual arose to articulate the beliefs of the group.

Articulation was often anonymous and transmitted in oral form by members of the community, who shaped and molded the theological expression with further insights. Additional confessions of faith elaborated the initial testimony, so that a cycle of traditions developed as each generation confessed the relevance of the event for its own situation. Finally, an editor fixed this developing process into written form, the layers of tradition stabilized into more fixed form and later changes appeared as simple editorial additions. The writings received increased respect as testimony to the faith, and finally they were placed into a canon. But even this was not the end, for the community of faith continued to use the text in meeting the needs of new situations, and new interpretations and traditions continued to arise even until today.

RISE OF THE CANON

The literature of the Old and New Testament grew slowly over the centuries and was brought together in unified form at various stages in the life of Israel and the Christian community. Usually a crisis or great social change caused literature to precipitate from its original oral form into literary form. This literature was created by the community of faith in order to preserve its self-understanding in the face of new social and religious problems. Scripture thus arises out of the need to address new problems by means of the old religious traditions. A canon or fixed corpus of literature takes shape because a question of identity or a challenge to authority has arisen, and only later does this literature become unchangeable once the question of identity has been settled.[1] Scripture arises in response to the needs of the community.

---

1. James Sanders, *Torah and Canon* (Philadelphia: Fortress, 1972), p. 91; and Joseph Blenkinsopp, *Prophecy and Canon: A Contribution to the Study of Jewish Origins* (Notre Dame: University Press, 1977), pp. 1–152.

Old Testament

The process which would eventually culminate in our Bible began with Israel. The Old Testament was shaped by the experience of Israel's destitution and transformation in the exile and post-exilic period, and, once created, it ultimately led Christians to create a parallel phenomenon, the New Testament. The process may be compared to a snowball rolling down a hill and gaining size along the way. The "snowball" which became the Bible had as its center certain core events, the exodus and resurrection experiences, both salvific actions of God. The literatures which accrued to the text were testimonies of human faith responding in greater or lesser measure to these foundational experiences.

The canon-making process may have begun in seventh century B.C. Judah with the Deuteronomic reform movement. Deuteronomic reformers drew upon the ancient laws and the oracles of the classical prophets to weave a Yahwistic vision of reform and invigoration for Judah in the later years of Josiah's reign (622–609 B.C.). This movement probably created the Books of Deuteronomy, Joshua, Judges, Samuel, and Kings as we now have them. Either they or subsequent editors attached the earlier Yahwistic and Elohistic traditions (Genesis, Exodus, Numbers) as a prelude to this Deuteronomistic history.[2] They have been called the creators of "legal scribalism" because they institutionalized the prior traditions and teachings of Israel into one grand scheme. They institutionalized the radical critique of the prophets by working prophetic values into the legal corpus of Deuteronomy and by subordinating all the prophets to the ultimate authority of Moses, the great lawgiver. This converted the living, charismatic, dynamic, oral "word" of the prophets into a written scribal, legal "word." Not only was this a step toward creating a canon, but it led to the equation of the "word of God" with torah and the eventual equation of both with Scripture.[3]

If the Deuteronomic reform movement did not initiate this process, most certainly the exilic theologians of the Babylonian exile (586–539

---

2. Childs, *Introduction to the Old Testament as Scripture* (Philadelphia: Fortress, 1979), pp. 60–67.

3. Grelot, "Tradition," p. 56; Blenkinsopp, *Prophecy,* pp. 24–53; and Barr, *Scope,* p. 117.

B.C.) are responsible. Under further Deuteronomic influence and Priestly contributions the Pentateuch and the prophetic corpus took shape. In this period prophetic material was brought together to emphasize salvation oracles over judgment oracles, for judgment was seen as past and the salvation was to be anticipated.[4] The prophetic corpus was subordinated to the Pentateuch, and the institutionalization of prophecy was complete.[5] Thus in exile a fuller canon began to emerge as an attempt by Jews to meet their theological problems.[6] At this stage the canon was a flexible and pluralistic document arising to offer a response to human existential need.[7]

The "canon" brought back from exile by the Jews enabled them to survive. For it was indestructible (unlike city, temple, or kings), it was made commonly available by copying, and it was portable and could be adopted by Jews scattered in diaspora as well as those in Judah. The process of canon growth continued in the exilic period. The last third of the Old Testament, created between 500 B.C. and 100 B.C., was recognized as Scripture by the early rabbis shortly after 100 A.D. Like the prophets this material was subordinated to the Pentateuch and may be called "scribal prophecy" (wisdom, novels, historiography, apocalyptic), a further institutionalized form of revelation.[8] In the post-exilic or second temple period Jews were becoming a people of the book, and for them the word of God increasingly became equated with written literature, the "Scriptures."

It is in this era that our common notion of inspiration arose. No longer seen as a charism bestowed upon living prophets, it became an attribute of the writings produced by the scribes. The literary transmission of prophecy provided Jews and Christians with the idea of scriptural inspiration, and this attribute was extended over literary works of a non-

4. Ronald Clements, "Patterns in the Prophetic Canon," *Canon and Authority,* pp. 42–55; and R. Rendtorff, *Das Alte Testament: Eine Einführung* (Neukirchen-Vluyn: Neukirchener, 1983), pp. 255–258.

5. J. McKenzie, "The Word of God in the Old Testament," *Myths and Realities,* p. 57; Vawter, *Inspiration,* p. 11; Blenkinsopp, *Prophecy,* pp. 24–53; and Barr, *Holy Scripture,* p. 11.

6. Sanders, *Torah,* p. 47.

7. Ibid., pp. ix–xx, 1–121, but p. 47 in particular, and "Adaptable for Life: The Nature and Function of Canon," *Magnalia Dei: The Mighty Acts of God,* ed. Frank Cross, Walter Lemke, and Patrick Miller (Garden City: Doubleday, 1976), pp. 531–552.

8. Sanders, "Adaptable," pp. 539–541; and Blenkinsopp, *Prophecy,* pp. 124–138.

prophetic nature. Though the dynamic aspect of inspiration was weakened, the books which inherited this charism became the mediator of God and religious meaning.[9]

The process of bringing literature together to form the canon was completed by Judaism after the holocaust of 70 A.D. The loss of Jerusalem and the temple along with the effective elimination of Jewish social-theological parties like the Sadducees, Zealots, and Essenes caused a crisis of identity. Out of this arose the Pharisaical-Rabbinic party to assume leadership. Under their direction the final Jewish canon took shape, although whether this was accomplished at the Council of Jabneh (also called Jamnia) is still disputed.[10]

Among early Christians the term "Scriptures" meant the loose collection of Old Testament writings prior to their consolidation as canon in the second century. Certainly the Pentateuch and prophets were accepted as "Scriptures," but the quotation of a wide range of literature by New Testament authors implies that early Christians considered many things to be "Scriptures" which were not accorded that status in the later years of the Church.

New Testament

The literature of the New Testament was written between 40 and 110. Oral tradition recalled the sayings and passion of Jesus until the distance from these events, the loss of eyewitnesses, and the needs of the Church necessitated the creation of Gospels by Mark, Matthew, Luke, and John (65–110). The earliest literature, Paul's epistles (45–65), had been recopied and preserved in the churches he had founded. Other writers imitated Pauline epistolary style, either under his name (Deutero-Pauline literature) or in terms of an address to churches at large (general or catholic epistles, 65–110).

Subsequent generations of Christians found this literature edifying and continued to use it. Church Fathers attest to the wide circulation of the four Gospels and the Pauline epistles; a less extensive usage is testified for the remaining material. Though debate exists as to whether these writ-

9. J. McKenzie, "Word of God," p. 57, and *Theology,* pp. 96–127, 130–132; Vawter, *Inspiration,* p. 11; and Grant, "Old Testament," p. 20, who points out that this period could experience the discussion of inspiration by someone like Philo, who saw the individual as an instrument of God, inspired to speak and write.

10. Turro and R.E. Brown, "Canonicity," p. 522; and Barr, *Holy Scripture,* p. 56.

ings were brought together in a cohesive fashion in the second or third centuries, testimonies of the Church Fathers do not imply the existence of a canon until the fourth century.[11] Even the Muratorian Fragment, once considered a second century document to prove an early existence for the canon, is viewed now as a fourth century list.[12] A growing consensus arose among Christians as to which books were most meaningful (certainly Paul and the Gospels), though there was no real agreement on the rest of the writings. The Old Testament writings were used by Christians as authoritative, perhaps because they explicated the prior assumption of the Jewish authors of New Testament writings and because the Jewish

---

11. Kurt Aland, *The Problem of the New Testament Canon,* Contemporary Studies in Theology, Vol. 7 (London: Mowbray, 1962), pp. 10–13; von Campenhausen, *The Formation of the Christian Bible,* trans. John Baker (Philadelphia: Fortress, 1972), pp. 103–326; Albert Sundberg, "The Making of the New Testament Canon," *The Interpreter's One Volume Commentary on the Bible,* ed. Charles Laymon (Nashville: Abingdon, 1971), pp. 1216–1224, and "Canon of the New Testament," *Interpreter's Dictionary of the Bible: Supplementary Volume,* ed. Keith Crim (Nashville: Abingdon, 1976), pp. 136–140; Barr, *Holy Scripture,* p. 50. Formerly scholars spoke of an "Alexandrian Canon" of the second and third centuries A.D., a hypothetical collection of Old Testament writings, but even this theory is being abandoned for the opinion that Christians collected Old Testament works late in the canon-making process along with the New Testament writings: Sundberg, *The Old Testament of the Early Church,* Harvard Theological Studies, Vol. 20 (Cambridge: Harvard University Press, 1964), pp. 3–176, "The Protestant Old Testament Canon: Should It Be Re-examined?" *Catholic Biblical Quarterly* 28 (1966): 194–203, "The 'Old Testament': A Christian Canon," *Catholic Biblical Quarterly* 30 (1968): 143–155, "New Testament Canon," pp. 1216–1217, and "Canon of the New Testament," pp. 136–137.

12. Sundberg, "The Old Testament of the Early Church," *Harvard Theological Review* 51 (1959): 205–226, "Toward a Revised History of the New Testament Canon," *Studia Evangelica* 4 (1968): 452–461, "New Testament Canon," pp. 1223–1224, "Canon Muratori: A Fourth-Century List," *Harvard Theological Review* 66 (1973): 1–41, "The Bible Canon and the Christian Doctrine of Inspiration," *Interpretation* 29 (1975): 352–371, and "Muratorian Fragment(s)," *Interpreter's Dictionary of the Bible: Supplementary Volume,* pp. 609–610. Primary sources may be evaluated in Frederik Grosheide, ed., *Some Early Lists of the Books of the New Testament,* Textus Minores, Vol. 1 (Leiden: Brill, 1948), pp. 5–24; the Muratorian fragment as listed on pp. 6–11. Sundberg notes the following about the Muratorian fragment: (1) *nuperrime* ("most recently") implies not that the writing, Shepherd of Hermas, was written recently, but rather it was the last document written of those under consideration, (2) the attitude toward Hermas reflects fourth century sensitivities, (3) the Wisdom of Solomon is mentioned in the New Testament canon, which means the Old Testament is considered to be closed by this time, (4) *urbis Romae* is a fourth century idiom; the second century idiom would have been *urbe Roma;* (5) *sedente cathedra urbis Romae ecclesiae* is a fourth century idiom, (6) the expression *ecclesia disciplina* was unknown in the second century, (7) Revelation was disputed in the fourth century debates, and (8) the Apocalypse of Peter was unknown in the West. Ergo, the Muratorian fragment was a fourth century Eastern document and not a second century Western document as we had traditionally maintained.

ethos helped Christians to maintain their identity in the face of Greek syncretizing heresies like Gnosticism and Docetism.

Canon as we have it was created in the fourth century in the wake of the Constantinian revolution, which brought hordes of converts into the churches. Canon was created for the purpose of organizing the teachings and the practice of the Church to accommodate this wave of incoming pagan converts. Discussion by leading theologians and decisions by Church councils at Hippo in 393 and Carthage in 397 and 419 produced our present canon with the list of contestable books known as *antilegoumena.*

Books were accepted into the canon because they agreed with the *regulum fidei* ("rule of faith"), the faith as articulated by Christians. Writings were not taken into the canon because of their quality of inspiration, for several works were considered to be inspired but not worthy of inclusion in the canon. Writings were accepted because they conformed to the faith as historically affirmed and practiced by Christians.[13] Many works had received great respect in prior centuries by Church Fathers such as Irenaeus, Tertullian, Origen, and others, because they were a good statement of the faith by which to oppose heresies like Gnosticism, Docetism, Montanism, and Marcion's activity. The Old Testament Scriptures were valid because they "predicted" Christ, and the "newer" Scriptures told directly of Christ's activities and passion.[14] This canon has been the heritage of the Christian Church for one and a half millennia.

IMPLICATIONS

The scholarly study of the growth of Scripture has several implications for our study. Most notably the concepts of canon, inspiration, and Scripture are affected.

The canon must now be viewed in more dynamic fashion. The canon developed gradually, the seeds of its inception were planted early, but

---

13. von Campenhausen, *Formation,* pp. 330–333; Turro and R.E. Brown, "Canonicity," p. 516; Sundberg, "New Testament Canon," pp. 1217, 1224, and "Canon of the New Testament," p. 137; and Everett Kalin, "The Inspired Community: A Glance at Canon History," *Concordia Theological Monthly* 42 (1971): 541–549.

14. Aland, *Problem,* pp. 18–24; von Campenhausen, *Formation,* pp. 103–133; especially pp. 327–333; and Maurice Wiles, "Origen as Biblical Scholar," *Cambridge History of the Bible,* 1:456.

the culmination of the process was late. Canonization was the final result of the formation of traditions. The entire process may be diagrammed as follows: Human Life Situation→ Traditions→ Corpus of Literature→ Sacred Texts→ Canon.[15] Throughout the process various steps were taken because of the social and religious needs of believers to articulate their self-understanding in the face of new problems which had arisen. Canon was a derivative of a greater process of creating traditions for theological expression. The canon was closed by the Church somewhat artificially in the fourth century, and for this reason the "edges" of the canon remain fuzzy. That is to say, some books within the canon do not seem to carry the same theological weight as others within the canon and even some outside the canon.[16] Such is the nature of an evolving process which moves according to the fabric of human religious and social needs. The end product may appear uneven. However, the quality of the canon is not to be judged by its systematic balance or cohesion but rather by the message it communicates in overall dynamic fashion.

To recognize this is not to deny the authority of the canon. The ancient Church did not bestow authority on the various works incorporated into the canon, it merely recognized the authority which already lay therein. The Church is subject to the canon of Scripture due to its theological importance for the expression of the faith. The Church is dependent upon the canon, and the creation of the canon was dependent upon the judgment of the Church. We have a paradoxical circle of authority.[17] As William Countryman says:

> The Scriptures which originated and were canonized in the community of faith now serve to judge the community, since they embody its earliest or best perception of its own essence.[18]

Viewed in this perspective the doctrine of Scripture is intertwined with the doctrine of the Church. If we understand Church as both Israel's community of faith as well as the ancient Christian community and Scrip-

---

15. Harmut Gese, "Tradition and Biblical Theology," *Tradition and Theology*, p. 317.

16. Kelsey, *Scripture*, pp. 100–108; and Barr, *Holy Scripture*, p. 63.

17. Aland, *Problem*, pp. 18–24; Burtchaell, *Catholic Theories*, pp. 300–304; Countryman, *Authority*, p. 70; Miller, "The Bible," pp. 103–104; and Bartlett, *Shape*, pp. 131–136.

18. Countryman, *Authority*, p. 70.

ture as the entire tradition-making process, we might say that Scripture and the Church developed together and mutually created each other. The doctrine of Scripture speaks about the divine presence with Israel and the ancient Church. The primary focus for describing the reality of Scripture lies with the formation of tradition. Only secondarily would Scripture refer to the process of fixing traditions into written form, for the actual writing of the texts is a minor function.[19]

Since Scripture arose out of the Church in a long process of oral tradition and written redaction, the traditional concept of inspiration loses its meaning. For the individual texts of Scripture were created by many nameless individuals in a group process. To speak of an inspired individual creating the text, as individual inspiration theories so often do, is absurd. If such a definition of inspiration is maintained, it becomes a very minor part of the process.[20]

If the concept of inspiration is to retain any meaning it must be viewed in the new light of this greater process. Wherein is inspiration in this process? It is found in the entire scope of creating the text and re-creating the primal experience for the community of faith. Inspiration occurs within the community; more than one individual can be said to be inspired. The community gives rise to oral traditions which precipitate into written Scripture. The inspiration process might be diagrammed as follows: God→ Community→ Tradition→ Scripture.[21] Inspiration occurs throughout the process as a driving force which leads to an ever changing and new re-expression of the faith. The moment of inspiration could be that point at which three elements are present: (1) reception of the old tradition, (2) application to a new situation, and (3) a respondent or theologian who applies the tradition to the new situation. This process of reinterpretation is inspiration, and the same inspiration which created the canon exists today as the text is relived in the community of faith.[22]

The doctrine of inspiration needs to be formulated in more dynamic fashion. James Barr has laid the foundation for the formulation in clear fashion. The primary locus of the doctrine concerns the formulation of doctrine in Israel and the early Church. Secondarily, it refers to the process of converting tradition into Scripture. (In this regard, many of the

19. Barr, *Fundamentalism*, p. 288.
20. Ibid., pp. 156, 288.
21. Kelsey, *Scripture*, pp. 32–119; and Barr, *Scope*, pp. 48, 60, 124–125.
22. Achtemeier, *Inspiration*, p. 114–147.

old formulations of the doctrine of inspiration were really concerned with the secondary aspect—the bookmaking process). The overarching principle which encompasses both aspects is the doctrine of divine providence—God dynamically guided the developed religious life of his people in Israel and the ancient Church.[23]

Wherein lies the authority of the Bible? The canon has authority because it is the spiritual life experience of the Church, the community of God both past and present. The canon contains the testimony to God's sanctification of a sinful people, a never-ending process throughout the lived experience of the race. The canon contains the paradigms of the divine process which are operative yet today.[24]

> The authority of Scripture is therefore demonstrated, not in the literary form in which it has been cast, as the supporters of inerrancy would have it, but rather in its power to create and shape reality.[25]

The authority of the Bible is a shared authority, for the paradox of the intertwined Scriptures and the community of faith implies that divine presence and binding authority lies in both. The authority of the Bible and the authority of the Church are one. The tradition and the community developed together, and in the final stages the Church defined the Scriptures as canon, yet ever since the Scriptures have been the norm for the Church's theology and traditions. The authority of the Bible and the Church are one, and they function in harmony when they reach out to meet human spiritual and physical needs. The Bible has authority to shape human existence.

But now we have come full cycle. The authority of the Bible lies in its power to shape our reality. We can sense it has that authority, and all are agreed to that premise. But have we really defined this authority? No! But then perhaps no definition, as the scholars have striven to offer, is really possible.

---

23. Barr, *Fundamentalism*, p. 288.
24. Hanson, "Contradiction," pp. 110–131; and Achtemeier, *Inspiration*, pp. 114–147.
25. Achtemeier, *Inspiration*, p. 159.

Chapter Fourteen

ECUMENICAL DISCUSSION: SCRIPTURE AND TRADITION

Modern biblical study has helped to bring about the ecumenical movement. The realization that diversity in the biblical community—Israel and the ancient Church—did not preclude unity then helped affirm the impetus toward cooperation between denominations today. More precise understanding of biblical concepts led many theologians to realize the artificial nature of some of their own traditional denominational statements, and this promoted a more cooperative spirit in ecumenical dialogue.

Ecumenical discussion has turned to the problem of biblical authority within recent years, and some insightful observations have been made. The World Council of Churches has turned its attention to this particular problem, and in particular the Faith and Order Conference at Montreal in 1963 gave consideration to this topic. The document which they produced formulated general views and defined several terms. "Tradition" was seen as the process of transmission—a process in both oral and written form which includes both the Bible and the living traditions of the Church. It refers to the ongoing growth of faith and theology within the living community of God. "Traditions" were seen as specific articulations of the faith community at various times in its history to express the faith in a particular form. "The tradition" refers to the revelation in Jesus Christ, the core of the faith. Tradition in the first sense was viewed as "the whole life of the Church," the process of faith affirmation which is undertaken in each new generation. The conference produced three resultant theses: (1) Scriptures are part of the tradition-making process, (2) Scriptures are interpreted in the light of "the tradition," and (3) Scriptures are the guardian of traditions and their supreme expression. These views represented the culmination of modern biblical and canon history scholarship. This definition mediates between Roman Catholic, Greek Orthodox, and Protestant positions. Though the centrality of the Bible for doing theology is affirmed, the weaknesses of a radical *sola scriptura* principle are admitted, for Scripture is viewed in an integral and inseparable relationship with tradition.[1] Among the delegates there was basic consensus that (1) the living word active in the Church is Jesus Christ, (2) *paradosis* ("that which is handed down" or tradition) is supremely found in the canon, though its authority was commissioned by Jesus Christ and begun before the creation of the canon, and (3) the Bible is the norm for continuing growth of tradition. The Bible is a confession and one is subject to its authority only by faith and conversion.[2]

The statements of this council also reflect the changes which have occurred among Roman Catholics and Protestants in the last generation. While Roman Catholics have turned more to the Scriptures in their scholarship in recent years, Protestants have relinquished their insistence upon *sola scriptura*. Catholics see tradition as deeply rooted in Scripture and as an on-going interpretation of Scripture, but no longer treat tradition as a source for theology equal to Scripture. Protestants have recognized the legitimacy of tradition; they have become more sensitive to the intellectual heritage of the Church prior to the Reformation.[3]

In the pre-Reformation Church the relationship between Scripture and tradition was never clearly defined. Theologians felt they were using Scripture as their norm, even when they were radically reinterpreting the text by their own religious and cultural values. For them Scripture and tradition were co-extensive; tradition was not viewed as a source of theology separate from Scripture; rather it was the proclaimed living Gospel interpreted anew by each generation.[4]

---

1. Bryant, *Authority*, pp. 95–96, 101–103; and Dulles, "Protestant and Catholic Views," p. 250.

2. Bryant, *Authority*, pp. 112, 161; and Rahner, *Inspiration*, pp. 40–86.

3. George Tavard, "The Authority of Scripture and Tradition," *Problems of Authority*, ed. John Todd (Baltimore: Helicon, 1962), pp. 27–42; and Dulles, "Catholic Perspective," p. 33.

4. Tavard, "Authority," p. 33; Grant, "The Creation of the Christian Tradition," p. 12, Robert McNally, "Christian Tradition and the Early Middle Ages," pp. 40–41, and "Tradition at the Beginning of the Reformation," pp. 75–76, *Perspectives on Scripture and Tradition*, ed. Joseph Kelly (Notre Dame: Fides, 1976), pp. 1–17, 37–83; and Vawter, "Bible," p. 117.

Roman Catholics first struggled with a definition for the relationship at the Council of Trent (1545–1563). They struggled with a definition which was rooted both in Scripture ("in part") and tradition ("in part")—*partim in libris scriptis partim in sine scripto traditionibus.* The mere existence of this formula in the discussion at Trent has served historically to undergird the famous two-source theory among many Roman Catholic theologians. The idea that Scripture and tradition were twin pillars of authority served as a polemic against the Protestant principle of *sola scriptura.* However, modern scholars have reminded us strongly that the Council of Trent rejected this formula and produced a significantly different statement—*in libris scriptis et sine scripto traditionibus.* They believe that Trent really rejected the two source theory of authority for a more unified view.[5] The two source theory developed in popular theology because of the particular work of Melchior Cano (1509–1560) in his *Loci theologici,* and in the writings of Peter Canisius (1521–1529) and Bellarmine (1542–1621).[6] Some modern Roman Catholics now speak bitterly of the two source theory:

> It was offensive; it degraded the majesty and authority of the divinely inspired word; and it neglected the consideration that scripture is from God; tradition from man. To equate the two is contrary to the sensus Christianus; worse still, it is blasphemy.[7]

Only a few theologians still speak cautiously of Trent's equal affirmation of tradition as authoritative for theology.[8]

Vatican II addressed the issue of Scripture and tradition anew. Vatican II spoke of "tradition" while Trent spoke of "traditions." Vatican II thus saw tradition as a unified whole, a fluid and dynamic process which underwent change and development for each new generation. Vatican II

---

5. This new interpretation is often associated with Geiselmann. Rahner, *Inspiration,* p. 36; Rahner and Ratzinger, *Revelation,* pp. 32–33; M. Barth, "Sola Scriptura," p. 76; Albert Outler, "Scripture, Tradition and Ecumenism," *Scripture and Ecumenism,* p. 9; McNally, "Reformation," p. 78; and Vawter, "Bible," p. 120.

6. Beegle, *Scripture,* pp. 102–103.

7. McNally, "Reformation," p. 78.

8. Rahner and Ratzinger, *Revelation,* pp. 65–66; the opinion expressed is that of Ratzinger.

broke with the two source theory, for Scripture and tradition were seen as a unified whole; both flow from the proclamation of the Gospel.[9]

The result has been an articulation on this issue by Roman Catholic theologians which is far more acceptable to Protestant theologians. Tradition is described as the presence of Christ in the faith of the Church manifesting itself anew for each generation. Tradition is an everflowing stream running through Church history to transmit the strength of the apostolic faith. Tradition makes Scripture available and understandable to a changing and imperfect world where the biblical text must be reinterpreted. Tradition is not a dogmatic appeal to the past but a selective process which draws upon meaningful insights, assesses them and interprets them anew.[10]

Such language appeals to the Protestant theologians. It destroys the old stereotype which perceived tradition as a substitute for Scripture in Roman Catholic theology. The view of tradition sounds like the Protestant understanding of the *viva vox,* the living voice of the preached word in the Church. Protestants also believe that modern Roman Catholics root tradition in the Scripture, and perhaps even subordinate it, as do they. Protestants rejected the elevation of tradition when it seemed to imply merely the total sum of Christian literature, but they are more comfortable with a definition which refers to dynamic preaching.[11]

Protestants, in turn, are giving up their radical insistence upon *sola scriptura.* The Scripture principle is not by definition opposed to tradition; rather for modern Protestants it is seen to undergird tradition. Scripture is authoritative for the Church and tradition, but Scripture and tradition both play a role in the formulation of theology. Scripture is something the Church has and uses to preserve its self-identity. Tradition is not something the Church uses, but something the Church is, which

---

9. Bea, *The Word of God and Mankind,* trans. Geoffrey Chapman (Chicago: Chapman, 1967), pp. 156–159; Tavard, "Tradition in Theology: A Problematic Approach," *Scripture and Tradition,* p. 96; Dulles, "Catholic Perspective," p. 35, and "Protestant and Catholic Views," p. 250.

10. Tavard, "Authority," p. 39, and "Approach," pp. 92–96; Rahner, *Investigations,* p. 151; and Rahner and Ratzinger, *Revelation,* pp. 37–49.

11. Tavard, "Authority," p. 33. This observation was first made by Johann von Kuhn, "Die formalen Principien des Katholicismus und Protestantismus," *Theologische Quartelschrift* 40 (1858): 1–62, cited in Burtchaell, *Catholic Theories,* p. 31.

refers to particular events, customs, and everyday practice that constitute churchly activity.[12]

Protestants have had to come to a number of painful realizations which led to this moderation. The debate over authority has led Protestants to realize that Scripture does not claim to be the exclusive source of faith, the unique deposit of revelation. *Sola scriptura* is not really taught in the Bible. The history of canon taught many Protestants that Scripture was a product of the community of faith, the Church. Previously they believed that the Bible came first historically and the Church developed upon its foundation. However, many now admit that the Church established the canon. Finally, Protestants have realized that in four hundred years they, too, have developed a "tradition" in each of their own denominations. To pretend that one interprets Scripture without a "tradition" or presuppositions makes one an unconscious slave to that "tradition." As Protestants began to assess critically their own respective traditions or presuppositions, they became more sympathetic to the greater "tradition" of the whole Christian experience. This has led them to understand the Roman Catholic views in more sympathetic fashion.[13]

Several Protestant theologians now speak of the relation of Scripture and tradition in ways which would be very compatible with Roman Catholic views. James Barr and David Kelsey both speak of the origin of Scripture in the tradition of the Church or the community of faith. Levels of authority are diagrammed as follows: God→ Church→ Tradition→ Scripture. Scripture is seen as the product of a tradition-making process which exists in the Church; the doctrines of Scripture and inspiration are "second-order" doctrines under the doctrine of the Church. Scripture's authority is really rooted in the authority of the Church and it is rooted ultimately in the authority of God.[14]

Protestant and Roman Catholic views need to complement each other. The Roman Catholic perspective which needs to be contributed is that tradition is a legitimate aspect of the theological endeavor. Scripture arose in the Church, in a tradition-making process. (It is interesting to note that the best advocates of a social inspiration model are Roman Cath-

---

12. M. Barth, "Sola Scriptura," p. 93; Kelsey, *Scripture,* pp. 96–100; and Dulles, "Protestant and Catholic Views," p. 250.
13. Tavard, "Authority," pp. 27–42; McNally, "Reformation," p. 74; Dulles, "Catholic Perspective," p. 33, and "Protestant and Catholic Views," p. 250; and Barr, *Holy Scripture,* pp. 26–27.
14. Kelsey, *Scripture,* p. 211; and Barr, *Scope,* pp. 48, 60.

olic.) The Protestant critiques are correct. Scripture is the primary source for doing theology. The later traditions must not dominate the Scriptures so as to prevent the message from being heard.[15]

However, despite the consensus certain nuances still remain to divide Christians. The World Council of Churches, meeting in 1963, became sensitive to these issues. The question arose concerning the source of authority for the proper interpretation of an authoritative Scripture. Wherein is vested the final authority to decide a debate on the interpretation of Scripture for a particular Church issue? Protestants would point to all ordained clergy, Greek Orthodox would submit to the hierarchy and Church councils, and Roman Catholics would defer to the bishops and the primate. The actual relationship between Scriptures and tradition was envisioned differently. Roman Catholics would view Christ as the ultimate authority, so that no real conflict should arise theoretically between Scriptures and tradition (George Tavard, Karl Rahner). Protestants saw Scripture as the initial core of a developing traditions process, so that Scripture remains the norm and corrective for tradition when the latter deviates from its authentic course (Karl Barth, Albert Outler, Wolfhart Pannenberg). Greek Orthodox viewed the Holy Spirit as the guiding authority, so the Scriptures and tradition are mystically united in him (Georges Florovsky, John Meyendorff, Panayotis Bratsiotis).[16]

Although a broad consensus has been established, not all the details have been worked out. The difficulty encountered is defining the relationship between the Bible and the later theological traditions of the Church, including the disparate traditions from respectively different denominations. Each denomination views the Bible through its own theological presuppositions or traditions, so that authority is not only in the Bible, but in the respective traditions of each denomination, whether they consciously admit it or not.

One notices among even progressive Roman Catholic views a tendency to reaffirm tradition over the Bible in new and subtle fashions. Among advocates of the social inspiration theory Scripture is subordinated to the inspired community or the Church. Advocates seem to imply that since the infallible teaching authority of the apostolic Church created Scripture, then the infallible teaching authority of the post-apostolic

---

15. Barr, *Holy Scripture,* pp. 28–29.

16. Bryant, *Authority,* pp. 82–83; Bratsiotis, "Orthodox Contribution," pp. 20–22; and Prenter, "Lutheran Contribution," pp. 110–111.

Church can interpret Scripture.[17] Statements to this effect can be found in Karl Rahner:

> The formation of the canon is a process whose legitimacy cannot be established by Scripture alone, but rather it is itself a fundamental movement in the tradition.[18]

> . . . because the Bible has been created from the beginning as the Scripture of the Church, and has in this way emerged as inspired, the mind of the Church has been adequately realized in the Scriptures.[19]

Perhaps the best way to respond to this is by using the World Council of Churches' definitions. A distinction was made between "the tradition" as the Gospel and "traditions" as specific articulations of the faith community. Perhaps the entire social inspiration model of Roman Catholic biblical scholars can be made far more compatible to Protestant sensitivities with this distinction. Scripture arises out of "the tradition" of the apostolic Church. Scripture in turn gives rise to "traditions" as the later Church must continually reinterpret the message for each new generation. Thus the scheme is as follows: The Tradition (Gospel)→ Scripture→ Traditions.[20] Such a model is in fact what many Protestant theologians have advocated. Traditions are subordinate to the Scripture (material principle of the faith), but the Scripture is subordinate to the Gospel it contains and proclaims (formal principle of the faith). This is what Protestant reformers meant when they spoke of *solus Christus* as a principle behind *sola scriptura*, as well as *sola gratia* and *sola fide*.

The debate, however, will not be settled by this author's contribution. The debate will continue because the ultimate difficulty lies in determining wherein is found true authority for the Christian Church.

Many scholars have noted the difficulty of declaring wherein the locus of authority resides, but they have maintained that it somehow lies in the relationship of the Bible and tradition. This tradition includes not

---

17. Rahner, *Inspiration*, p. 72; and J. McKenzie, "Inspiration," p. 390.
18. Rahner, *Foundations*, p. 376.
19. Rahner, *Inspiration*, p. 36.
20. Congar, *La Tradition et les traditiones: essai historique* (Paris: Fayard, 1960), pp. 13–33 et passim.

only the official theology of the Church, but also human conscience, reason, liturgical practice, and personal communion with God. Together all these forces affect each other and the believers to impress upon them the authority of the Bible. These other factors draw upon the Bible for authority, but in turn they give it validity. The Church created the canon, yet the message found therein created and still regulates the Church. A circle of interdependence is the source of authority.[21]

As Roman Catholics and Protestants dialogue with each other, they ask difficult questions. Protestants ask whether the Scripture can be turned over to the Church without losing its power and vitality under the direction of the magisterium and undisciplined growth of the *sensus fidelium* ("sense of the faithful believers" for the theology and practice in the everyday life of the Church). Roman Catholics ask whether the Scriptures can be used without leaving the Church at the mercy of exegetes, historians, and critical theologians who might lead the Church in such a new direction as to turn its back on much of the Christian tradition.[22] Roman Catholics in particular struggle to find a new locus for positing authority. As Karl Rahner says:

> . . . if we decide for the Bible, we do not know where to find its binding character; if we decide for the authority of the Church, we can hardly maintain authoritative writings beside it.[23]

The consensus of the World Council of Churches and the increased sensitivity to the complexity of these issues has arisen in part as a result of the modern critical investigation of the Scriptures and canon. Scholars have been led to transcend the narrow articulations of their own respective

---

21. Bratsiotis, "Orthodox Contribution," pp. 20–22; Clarence Tucker Craig, "A Methodist Contribution," *Symposium*, pp. 32–35; Dodd, "Relevance," p. 157; Florovsky, "Revelation," p. 164; Muilenburg, "Interpretation," p. 216; John Burnaby, "Bible and Dogma," *Recent Studies*, pp. 33–47 = *Church Quarterly Review* 159 (1958): 179–192; Evans, "Inspiration," pp. 25–31, and "Bible and Tradition," *Recent Studies*, pp. 72–80 = *Theology* 60 (1957): 437–444; Nineham, "Authority," pp. 81–96; Mickelsen, "Authority," pp. 77–105; Ramm, "Essence," pp. 112–113; and Hanson, "Contradiction," p. 131.

22. Rahner and Ratzinger, *Revelation*, p. 31. R.M. Brown, "Karl Barth," p. 42, points out that Barth asks the Roman Catholic question of his fellow Protestants—can they take tradition seriously?

23. Rahner, *Inspiration*, p. 32.

denominations, and they have become more aware of perspectives in the text which have been appropriated by denominations other than their own, so that they realized that no one denomination had a monopoly on biblical theology. More importantly they perceived the diversity of theology in the text, a clear testimony to the fact that such theological diversity has always been a hallmark of the greater Church, and causes for denominational strife are wanting. Church unity proceeds from plurality, not uniformity. Finally, they learned to appreciate the subtle interplay between the creation of the text and the community of faith and how the biblical text itself was a compilation of an ongoing traditions development. But in this great new age of self-discovery we are not sure where the future lies for understanding the Bible, tradition, and the Church.

Chapter Fifteen

CONCLUSION

Our review of models for understanding the authority of Scripture and the theologians who endorse them has probably not solved the debate. It has merely reviewed the quest for authority in an effort to awaken others to the possibility of undertaking their own quest. Even if no ultimate answer can be found, the toil and research and contemplation will provide valuable rewards for those who study the problem.

This work has tried to unfold the diversity of opinion on the issue of biblical authority. Perhaps this may explain the diversity of theology to be found in the Christian Church. When theologians do different things in their methodologies for interpreting Scripture, they have different concepts of biblical authority underlying their theology. But all theologians have certain principles in common: (1) They believe that theology should somehow appeal to biblical texts, even if only in a limited fashion. (2) Scriptures are perceived as normative in some form; they provide guidelines or a range of possibilities for doing theology. (3) The use of Scripture makes one's theology part of the greater Christian tradition.[1] Beyond that theologians may exhibit great diversity.

The models we have considered are arbitrary creations by this author. Certainly one could realign the categories in different fashion. The categories could almost be reduced to two large divisions—the objective assertative models and the non-informative expressive models. Theories such as strict and limited verbal inspiration, idea inspiration, social inspiration, salvation history, and Christocentric models tend to work with an objective principle that finds Scripture affecting theological statements with meaningful religious assertions. Theories such as inspiration of the

---

1. Kelsey, *Scripture,* pp. 147–153, 196–197.

original speaker, all existential models, and some of the theories of limited authority emphasize the expressive communication of scriptural experiences in subjective fashion to affect present human behavior. In reality, Scripture functions in both fashions in the life of the Church.[2] Different theologians will emphasize either the objective or the subjective side according to the theological tradition in which they were trained and their own personal inclination. Perhaps in this regard we might admit that truth is found in every position we have discussed. There are many ways to the center, and each theologian has chosen his or her own path.

Perhaps a new consensus will arise in viewing biblical authority, or perhaps we shall learn to admit that no one model can adequately answer all the problems. This author is torn between trying to draw an eclectic theory out of many of the models on the one hand, and simply declaring that it is impossible to articulate any theory by which to understand biblical authority in its fullest sense. The consensus of scholars who have engaged in the study of this issue seems to lie with the latter option.

Kelsey seems to give the best answer which can be given at this present point:

> Taking these writings as "scripture," and even as "canon," is an integral part of becoming a Christian. . . . To adopt the "canon" as "authority" for the common life of the church is to adopt, for whatever reasons, the particular way of being "Christian" that much of the ancient church also adopted.[3]

Scripture is authoritative—by that we mean that it provides insight for the Church on how to be Christian in word and deed, and it provides a pattern by which the Church adapts its life style to each new generation. Scripture is authoritative because of what it does for the Church, not because of what it is; it provides us with our Christian identity. The Scriptures are authoritative because the Church has chosen to use them for two thousand years.[4]

William Countryman has spoken in almost poetic fashion of the Bible as a document for a pilgrim people, the Church, who have wandered through time and space. The Bible is not an absolute authority; it is only

---

2. Ibid., pp. 148–151.
3. Ibid., pp. 164–165; and Bartlett, *Shape,* pp. 2–3, affirms the same idea.
4. Kelsey, *Scripture,* pp. 89–94, 194–196; and Barr, *Scope,* pp. 52, 111–138.

one of the authorities which God has given to us along with other institutions in the Church. This pilgrim document we call the Bible accompanies us on our journey through the millennia. It offers new perspectives to shake us out of old fixed patterns so that we might meet the continually ever new and present crises which face us on our earthly sojourn. The Bible is not the absolute authority; only God can be that.[5]

As God is beyond our reach, perhaps a final definition of biblical authority will remain beyond our reach. Certainly we desire authority for the sake of order in our corporate and individual lives. In this existence perhaps no absolute definition of biblical authority can exist, and we must learn to accept that. We must let go and trust with simple faith in the only absolute authority, God.

5. Countryman, *Authority*, pp. 9–110; and Barr, *Scope*, pp. 48, 60.

BIBLIOGRAPHY: WORKS CITED

Abraham, William. *The Divine Inspiration of Holy Scripture*. Oxford, England: University Press, 1981.

Achtemeier, Paul. *The Inspiration of Scripture: Problems and Proposals*. Biblical Perspectives on Current Issues. Philadelphia: Westminster, 1980.

Ackroyd, Peter; Evans, Christopher; Lampe, Geoffrey; and Greenslade, Stanley, eds. *Cambridge History of the Bible*. 3 vols. Cambridge, England: University Press, 1963–1970.

Aland, Kurt. *The Problem of the New Testament Canon*. Contemporary Studies in Theology, Vol. 7. London: Mowbray, 1962.

Alexander, Archibald. *Evidences of the Authenticity, Inspiration, and Canonical Authority of the Holy Scriptures*. Philadelphia: Presbyterian Board of Publication, 1836.

Alley, Robert. *Revolt Against the Faithful: A Biblical Case for Inspiration as Encounter*. New York: Lippincott, 1970.

Alonso-Schökel, Luis. "Hermeneutics in the Light of Language and Literature." *Catholic Biblical Quarterly* 25 (1963): 371–386.

———. *The Inspired Word: Scripture in the Light of Language and Literature*. Trans. Francis Martin. New York: Herder and Herder, 1972.

Althaus, Paul. *The Theology of Martin Luther*. Trans. Robert Schultz. Philadelphia: Fortress, 1966.

Anderson, George. "Canonical and Non-Canonical," *Cambridge History of the Bible*, Vol. 1.

Archer, Gleason. "Alleged Errors and Discrepancies of the Bible," *Inerrancy*. Ed. Geisler.

———. "The Witness of the Bible to Its Own Inerrancy." *Foundations of Biblical Authority*. Ed. Boice.

Bahnsen, Greg. "The Inerrancy of the Autographa." *Inerrancy*. Ed. Geisler.

Barr, James. *The Bible in the Modern World*. New York: Harper and Row, 1973.

———. *Fundamentalism*. Philadelphia: Westminster, 1978.

———. *Holy Scripture: Canon, Authority, Criticism*. Philadelphia: Westminster, 1983.

———. "The Interpretation of Scripture. II. Revelation Through History in the Old Testament and in Modern Theology." *Interpretation* 17 (1963): 193–205.

———. *The Scope and Authority of the Bible*. Philadelphia: Westminster, 1980.

Barth, Karl. *Church Dogmatics*. Vol. 1: *The Doctrine of the Word of God*. Trans. Geoffrey Bromiley. Ed. Geoffrey Bromiley and Thomas Torrance. Edinburgh: Clark, 1956.

———. *The Word of God and the Word of Man*. Trans. Douglas Morton. New York: Harper, 1957.

Barth, Markus. *Conversation with the Bible*. New York: Holt, Rinehart, and Winston, 1964.

———. "Sola Scripture." *Scripture and Ecumenism*. Ed. Swidler.

Bartlett, David. *The Shape of Scriptural Authority*. Philadelphia: Fortress, 1983.

Bea, Augustin. *De inspiratione et inerrantia sacrae scripturae*. Rome: Pontifical Biblical Institute, 1954.

———. *The Word of God and Mankind*. Trans. Geoffrey Chapman. Chicago: Franciscan, 1967.

Beegle, Dewey. *The Inspiration of Scripture*. Philadelphia: Westminster, 1963.

———. *Scripture, Tradition, and Infallibility*. Grand Rapids: Eerdmans, 1973.

Benoit, Pierre. "The Analogies of Inspiration." *Aspects of Biblical Inspiration*. = "Les analogies de l'inspiration." *Sacra Pagina*, 1:86–99. Ed. Coppens. = *Exegese et Theologie*, 3:17–30.

———. *Aspects of Biblical Inspiration*. Trans. Jerome Murphy-O'Connor and S.K. Ashe. Chicago: Priory, 1965.

———. *Exegese et Theologie*. 3 vols. Paris: Cerf, 1961–1968.

———. *Inspiration and the Bible*. Trans. Jerome Murphy-O'Connor and M. Keverne. New York: Sheed and Ward, 1965.

———. "Inspiration and Revelation." *The Human Reality of Sacred Scripture*. Concilium, Vol. 10. New York: Paulist, 1965.

————. "La Septante est-elle inspiree?" *Vom Wort des Lebens*. Munster: West, 1951. = *Exegese et Theologie*, 1:3–12.

————. "L'inspiratione des Septante d'apres les Peres." *L'homme devant Dieu*. = *Exegese et Theologie*, 3:69–89.

————. "Note complementaire sur l'inspiration." *Revue biblique* 63 (1956): 416–422.

————. "Revelation and Inspiration." *Aspects of Biblical Inspiration*. = "Revelation et inspiration selon la Bible, chez saint Thomas et dans la sainte Ecriture." *Revue biblique* 70 (1963): 321–370. = *Exegese et Theologie*, 3:90–142.

Berkouwer, Gerrit. *Holy Scripture*. Grand Rapids: Eerdmans, 1975.

Blank, Sheldon. "The Hebrew Scriptures as a Source for Moral Guidance." *Perspectives in the Jewish and Christian Traditions*. Ed. Greenspahn.

Blenkinsopp, Joseph. *Prophecy and Canon: A Contribution to the Study of Jewish Origins*. Notre Dame: University Press, 1977.

Bloesch, Donald. "The Primacy of Scripture." *Authoritative Word*, Ed. McKim. = *Essentials of Evangelical Theology*. Vol. 1: *God, Authority, and Salvation*. New York: Harper and Row, 1978.

Boice, James Montgomery, ed. *The Foundations of Biblical Authority*. Grand Rapids: Zondervan, 1978.

Bratsiotis, Panayotis. "An Orthodox Contribution." *Biblical Authority for Today: Symposium*. Eds. Richardson and W. Schweitzer.

Bright, John. *The Authority of the Old Testament*. Grand Rapids: Baker, 1967.

Brown, Raymond E., Fitzmyer, Joseph, and Murphy, Roland, eds. *Jerome Biblical Commentary*. Englewood Cliffs: Prentice-Hall, 1968.

Brown, Robert McAfee. "Scripture and Tradition in the Theology of Karl Barth." *Scripture and Ecumenism*. Ed. Swidler.

Brunner, Emil. *Revelation and Reason*. Trans. Olive Wyon. Philadelphia: Westminster, 1946.

Bryant, Robert. *The Bible's Authority Today*. Minneapolis: Augsburg, 1968.

Bultmann, Rudolf. "General Truths and Christian Proclamation to Friedrich Gogarten on His 70th Birthday." Trans. Schubert Ogden. *History and Hermeneutic*. Eds. Funk and Ebeling.

————. *Jesus Christ and Mythology*. New York: Scribner's, 1958.

————. "Preaching: Genuine and Secularized." *Religion and Culture:*

Essays in Honor of Paul Tillich. Ed. Walter Leibrecht. New York: Harper and Row, 1959.

―――. *Theology of the New Testament.* Trans. Kenrick Grobel. New York: Scribners, 1955.

Burnaby, John. "Bible and Dogma." *Some Recent Studies. = Church Quarterly Review* 159 (1958): 179–192.

Burtchaell, James Tunstead. *Catholic Theories of Biblical Inspiration since 1810: A Review and Critique.* Cambridge, England: University Press, 1969.

von Campenhausen, Hans. *The Formation of the Christian Bible.* Trans. John Baker. Philadelphia: Fortress, 1972.

―――. "Das Problem der Ordnung im Urchristentum und in der Alten Kirche." *Tradition und Leben.* Tübingen: Mohr, 1962.

Carnell, Edward John. *The Case for Orthodox Theology.* Philadelphia: Westminster, 1959.

Carson, D.A., and Woodbridge, John, eds. *Scripture and Truth.* Grand Rapids: Zondervan, 1983.

Childs, Brevard. *Biblical Theology in Crisis.* Philadelphia: Westminster, 1970.

―――. *Introduction to the Old Testament as Scripture.* Philadelphia: Fortress, 1979.

Clements, Ronald. "Patterns in the Prophetic Canon." *Canon and Authority.* Eds. Coats and Long.

Coats, George, and Long, Burke, eds. *Canon and Authority: Essays in Old Testament Religion and Theology.* Philadelphia: Fortress, 1977.

Coleman, Richard. "Biblical Inerrancy: Are We Going Anywhere?" *Theology Today* 33 (1976): 295–303.

Congar, Yves. "Inspiration des ecritures canoniques et apostolicite de l'Eglise." *Revue des Sciences Philosophiques et Theologiques* 45 (1961): 32–42.

―――. *La Tradition et les traditiones: Essai Historique.* Paris: Fayard, 1960.

Coppens, Joseph. "Comment mieux concevoir et énoncer l'inspiration et l'inerrance des Saintes Ecritures?" *Nouvelle Revue Theologique* 86 (1964): 933–947.

―――. Descamps, Albert, and Massaux, Edouard. *Sacra Pagina: Miscellanea Biblica Congressus Internationalis Catholici de Re Bib-*

lica. Bibliotheca Ephemeridum Theologicarum Lovaniensium, Vols. 12–13. Gembloux: Duculot, 1959.

Countryman, William. *Biblical Authority or Biblical Tyranny?* Philadelphia: Fortress, 1981.

Craig, Clarence Tucker. "A Methodist Contribution." *Biblical Authority for Today: Symposium.* Eds. Richardson and W. Schweitzer.

Crehan, F. J. "The Bible in the Roman Catholic Church from Trent to the Present Day." *Cambridge History of the Bible,* Vol. 3.

Crim, Keith, ed. *Interpreter's Dictionary of the Bible: Supplementary Volume.* Nashville: Abingdon, 1976.

Cullmann, Oscar. *Christ and Time.* Trans. Floyd Filson. Philadelphia: Westminster, 1964.

Cunliffe-Jones, Hubert. *The Authority of the Biblical Revelation.* Boston: Pilgrim, 1948.

———. "A Congregationalist Contribution." *Biblical Authority for Today: Symposium.* Eds. Richardson and W. Schweitzer.

Curtis, Olin. *The Christian Faith.* London: Eaton and Mains, 1905.

Davis, John Jefferson. "Genesis, Inerrancy, and the Antiquity of Man." *Inerrancy and Common Sense.* Eds. Nicole and Michaels.

Davis, Stephan. *The Debate about the Bible: Inerrancy versus Infallibility.* Philadelphia: Westminster, 1977.

Devadutt, Vinjamuri. "A Baptist Contribution." *Biblical Authority for Today: Symposium.* Eds. Richardson and W. Schweitzer.

DeWolf, Harold. *A Theology of the Living Church.* New York: Harper and Row, 1953.

Dinkler, Erich. *Bibelauthorität und Bibelkritik.* Sammlung Gemeinverständlicher Vorträge und Schriften aus dem Gebiet der Theologie und Religionsgeschichte, Vol. 193. Tübingen: Mohr, 1950.

Dodd, Charles Harold. *The Authority of the Bible.* Rev. ed. London: Fontana, 1960.

———. "The Relevance of the Bible." *Biblical Authority for Today: Symposium.* Eds. Richardson and W. Schweitzer.

Dulles, Avery. "The Authority of Scripture: A Catholic Perspective." *Scripture in the Jewish and Christian Traditions.* Ed. Greenspahn.

———. "Scripture: Recent Protestant and Catholic Views." *Authoritative Word.* Ed. McKim.

———. "The Theology of Revelation." *Theological Studies* 25 (1964): 43–58.

Elert, Werner. *The Structure of Lutheranism*. Trans. Walter Hanson. St. Louis: Concordia, 1962.

Elliot, John. "The New Testament Is Catholic: A Re-evaluation of Sola Scriptura." *Una Sancta* 23 (1966): 3–19.

Elze, Martin. *Tatian und seine Theologie*. Forschungen zur Kirchen- und Dogmengeschichte, Vol. 9. Göttingen: Vandenhoeck und Ruprecht, 1960.

Engelder, Theodore. *Scripture Cannot Be Broken: Six Objections to Verbal Inspiration Examined in the Light of Scripture*. St. Louis: Concordia, 1944.

Evans, Christopher. "Bible and Tradition." *Some Recent Studies. = Theology* 60 (1957): 437–444.

———. "The Inspiration of the Bible." *Some Recent Studies. = Theology* 59 (1956): 11–17.

Farley, Edward. *Ecclesial Man: A Social Phenomenology of Faith and Reality*. Philadelphia: Fortress, 1975.

Farrar, Austin. *The Glass of Vision*. London: n.p., 1948.

———. *A Rebirth of Images*. London: n.p., 1949.

———. *St. Matthew and St. Mark*. London: n.p., 1954.

———. *A Study in St. Mark*. London: n.p., 1951.

Feinberg, Paul. "The Meaning of Inerrancy." *Inerrancy*. Ed. Geisler.

Florovsky, Georges. "Revelation and Interpretation." *Biblical Authority for Today: Symposium*. Ed. Richardson and W. Schweitzer.

Forestell, Terrence. "Bible II (Inspiration)." *New Catholic Encyclopedia*. 17 vols. New York: McGraw-Hill, 1967.

———. "The Limitation of Inerrancy." *Catholic Biblical Quarterly* 20 (1958): 9–18.

Fosdick, Harry Emerson. *A Guide to Understanding the Bible*. New York: Harper and Brothers, 1938.

———. *The Modern Use of the Bible*. New York: Macmillan, 1924.

Funk, Robert, and Ebeling, Gerhard. *History and Hermeneutic*. Trans. Paul Achtemeier. Journal for Theology and the Church, Vol. 4. New York: Harper and Row, 1967.

Gaussen, Louis. *The Inspiration of the Holy Scriptures*. Trans. David Scott. London: Farncombe and Son, 1912.

Geiselmann, Rupert. *The Meaning of Tradition*. Quaestiones Disputatae, Vol. 15. New York: Herder and Herder, 1966.

Geisler, Norman, ed. *Inerrancy*. Grand Rapids: Zondervan, 1979.

Gerstner, John. "The Church's Doctrine of Biblical Inspiration." *Foundations of Biblical Authority*. Ed. Boice.

———. "A Protestant View of Biblical Authority." *Scripture in the Jewish and Christian Traditions*. Ed. Greenspahn.

———. "The View of the Bible Held by the Church: Calvin and the Westminster Divines." *Inerrancy*. Ed. Geisler.

———. "Warfield's Case for Biblical Inerrancy." *God's Inerrant Word*. Ed. Montgomery.

Gese, Hartmut. "Tradition and Biblical Theology." *Tradition and Theology*. Ed. Knight.

Gogarten, Friedrich. "Theology and History." Trans. Louis De Grazia. *History and Hermeneutic*. Eds. Funk and Ebeling.

Grant, Robert. "The Creation of the Christian Tradition." *Perspectives on Scripture and Tradition*. Ed. Kelly.

———. "Jesus and the Old Testament." *Authoritative Word*. Ed. McKim.

Greenspahn, Frederick, ed. *Scripture in the Jewish and Christian Traditions: Authority, Interpretation, Relevance*. Nashville: Abingdon, 1982.

Grelot, Pierre. "Tradition as Source and Environment of Scripture." Trans. Theodore Westow. *The Dynamism of Biblical Tradition*. Concilium, Vol. 20. New York: Paulist, 1967.

Grosheide, Frederik Willem, ed. *Some Early Lists of the Books of the New Testament*. Textus Minores, Vol. 1. Leiden: Brill, 1948.

Grudem, Wayne. "Scripture's Self-Attestation and the Problem of Formulating a Doctrine of Scripture." *Scripture and Truth*. Eds. Carson and Woodbridge.

Hagglund, Bengt. *History of Theology*. Trans. Gene Lund. St. Louis: Concordia, 1968.

Hanson, Paul. "The Theological Significance of Contradiction within the Book of the Covenant." *Canon and Authority*. Ed. Coats and Long.

von Harnack, Adolf. *What Is Christianity?* Trans. Thomas Bailey Saunders. New York: Harper and Row, 1957.

Harrington, Wilfrid. *Key to the Bible*. Vol. 1: *Record of Revelation*. Garden City: Doubleday, 1976.

———. *Record of Revelation: The Bible*. Chicago: Priory, 1965.

Heidt, William. *Inspiration, Canonicity, Texts, Versions, Hermeneu-*

tics—*A General Introduction to Sacred Scripture*. Old Testament Reading Guide, Vol. 31. Collegeville, Minnesota: Liturgical Press, 1970.

Henry, Carl. *God, Revelation and Authority*. Vol. 2: *God Who Speaks and Shows*. Waco, Texas: Word, 1976.

Herbert, Gabriel. *The Authority of the Old Testament*. London: Faber and Faber, 1947.

Hodge, Archibald Alexander. *Outline of Theology*. Grand Rapids: Eerdmans, 1949. (Reprint of 1897 ed.)

———, and Warfield, Benjamin Breckenridge, "Inspiration." *The Presbyterian Review* 7 (1881): 225–260.

Hodge, Charles. *Systematic Theology*. 3 vols. New York: Scribner's, 1899.

———. "What Is Christianity?" *The Biblical Repertory and Princeton Review* (1860).

Hodgson, Leonard. "God and the Bible." *Some Recent Studies.* = *Church Quarterly Review* 159 (1958): 532–546.

Hoffman, Thomas. "Inspiration, Normativeness, Canonicity, and the Unique Sacred Character of the Bible." *Catholic Biblical Quarterly* 44 (1982): 447–469.

Hubbard, David. "The Current Tensions: Is There a Way Out?" *Biblical Authority*. Ed. Rogers.

Jensen, Robert. "On the Problem(s) of Scriptural Authority." *Interpretation* 31 (1977): 237–250.

Johnston, Robert. *Evangelicals at an Impasse: Biblical Authority in Practice*. Atlanta: Knox, 1979.

Jones, Alexander. "Biblical Inspiration: A Christian Rendezvous?" *Scripture* 10 (1958): 97–109.

Käsemann, Ernst. "Is the Gospel Objective?," "Ministry and Community in the New Testament," "The Canon of the New Testament and the Unity of the Church," and "Apologia for Primitive Christian Eschatology." *Essays on New Testament Themes*. Trans. William John Montague. Studies in Biblical Theology, Vol. 41. London: SCM, 1964.

———. "Paul and Early Catholicism," and "Unity and Multiplicity in the New Testament Doctrine of the Church." *New Testament Questions of Today*. Trans. William John Montague and Wilfrid Bunge. Philadelphia: Fortress, 1969.

Kähler, Martin. *The So-Called Historical Jesus and the Historic, Biblical Christ.* Trans. Carl Braaten. Philadelphia: Fortress, 1964.

Kalin, Everett. "The Inspired Community: A Glance at Canon History." *Concordia Theological Monthly* 42 (1971): 541–549.

Kaufman, Gordon. "What Shall We Do with the Bible?" *Interpretation* 25 (1971): 95–112.

Kelly, Joseph, ed. *Perspectives on Scripture and Tradition.* Notre Dame: Fides, 1976.

Kelsey, David. "Protestant Attitudes Regarding Methods of Biblical Interpretation." *Scripture in Jewish and Christian Traditions.* Ed. Greenspahn.

———. *The Uses of Scripture in Recent Theology.* Philadelphia: Fortress, 1975.

Kierkegaard, Soren. "Of the Difference between a Genius and an Apostle" (1847). *The Present Age.* Oxford, England: University Press, 1940.

Knight, Douglas. *Tradition and Theology in the Old Testament.* Philadelphia: Fortress, 1977.

Knox, John. *The Church and the Reality of Christ.* New York: Harper and Row, 1962.

———. *The Early Church and the Coming Great Church.* Nashville: Abingdon, 1955.

Koch, Klaus. "Die Eigenart der priesterschriften Sinaigesetzgebung." *Zeitschrift für Theologie und Kirche* 55 (1958): 36–51.

Kraus, Hans Joachim. *Geschichte der historisch-kritischen Erforschung des Alten Testaments.* 2nd ed. Neukirchen-Vluyn: Neukirchener, 1969.

Kümmel, Werner Georg. "Notwendigkeit und die Grenze des neutestamentlichen Kanons." *Zeitschrift für Theologie und Kirche* 47 (1950): 277–313.

Küng, Hans. " 'Early Catholicism' in the New Testament as a Problem in Controversial Theology." *The Council in Action.* Trans. Cecil Hastings. New York: Sheed and Ward, 1963.

———. *Structures of the Church.* South Bend: Notre Dame, 1968.

Latourelle, Rene. *Theology of Revelation.* Staten Island: Alba, 1966.

Laurin, Robert. "Tradition and Canon." *Tradition and Theology.* Ed. Knight.

L'homme devant Dieu: Melanges offerts au Pere Henri du Lubac, S.J. 3 vols. Paris: Aubier, 1963.

Lightner, Robert. *The Saviour and the Scriptures: A Case for Scriptural Inerrancy.* Grand Rapids: Baker, 1966.

Lindblom, Johannes. *Prophecy in Ancient Israel.* Philadelphia: Fortress, 1973.

Lindsell, Harold. *The Battle for the Bible.* Grand Rapids: Zondervan, 1976.

Lohfink, Norbert. "The Inerrancy and the Unity of Scripture." *Modern Biblical Studies.* Eds. McCarthy and Callen. = Über die Irrtumlosigkeit und die Einheit der Schrift." *Stimmen der Zeit* 174 (1964): 161–181.

––––––. "The Truth of the Bible and Historicity." *Modern Biblical Studies.* Eds. McCarthy and Callen. = "Die Wahrheit der Bibel und die Geschichtlichkeit der Evangelien." *Orientierung* 29 (1965): 254–256.

Loretz, Oswald. *The Truth of the Bible.* Trans. David Bourke. New York: Herder, 1968.

Lovelace, Richard. "Inerrancy: Some Historical Perspectives." *Inerrancy and Common Sense.* Eds. Nicole and Michaels.

McBrien, Richard. "Catholicism as an Integrationist Perspective." *Scripture in the Jewish and Christian Traditions.* Ed. Greenspahn.

McCarthy, Dennis. "Personality, Society, and Inspiration." *Modern Biblical Studies.* Eds. McCarthy and Callen. = *Theological Studies* 24 (1963): 553–576.

McCarthy, Dennis, and Callen, William. *Modern Biblical Studies.* Milwaukee: Bruce, 1967.

McKenzie, John. "Inspiration." *Dictionary of the Bible.* New York: Macmillan, 1965.

––––––. *Myths and Realities: Studies in Biblical Theology.* Milwaukee: Bruce, 1963.

––––––. *The Old Testament Without Illusions.* Chicago: Thomas More, 1979.

––––––. "The Social Character of Inspiration." *Myths and Realities.* = *Catholic Biblical Quarterly* 24 (1962) 115–124.

––––––. *A Theology of the Old Testament.* Garden City: Doubleday, 1976.

————. *The Two-Edged Sword: An Interpretation of the Old Testament*. Garden City: Doubleday, 1956.

————. "The Word of God in the Old Testament." *Myths and Realities*. = *Theological Studies* 21 (1960): 183–206.

McKenzie, Roderick. "Some Problems in the Field of Inspiration." *Catholic Biblical Quarterly* 20 (1958): 1–8.

McKim, Donald, ed. *The Authoritative Word: Essays on the Nature of Scripture*. Grand Rapids: Eerdmans, 1983.

McNally, Robert. "Christian Tradition and the Early Middle Ages." *Perspectives on Scripture and Tradition*. Ed. Kelly.

————. "Tradition at the Beginning of the Reformation." *Perspectives on Scripture and Tradition*. Ed. Kelly.

McPherson, Dave. *The Incredible Cover-Up: The True Story of the Pre-Trib Rapture*. Plainfield, New Jersey: Logos, 1975.

Marsh, John. "History and Interpretation." *Biblical Authority for Today: Symposium*. Eds. Richardson and W. Schweitzer.

Marxsen, Willi. *Der Frühkatholizimus in Neuen Testament*. Neukirchen: Neukirchener, 1958.

Meyendorff, John. "The Meaning of Tradition." *Scripture and Ecumenism*. Ed. Swidler.

Michaels, Ramsey. "Inerrancy or Verbal Inspiration? An Evangelical Dilemma." *Inerrancy and Common Sense*. Ed. Nicole and Michaels.

Michl, Johann. "Scripture." *Encyclopedia of Biblical Theology*. Ed. Johannes Bauer. New York: Crossroad, 1981.

Mickelsen, Berkeley. "The Bible's Own Approach to Authority." *Biblical Authority*. Ed. Rogers.

Miller, Donald. "The Bible." *Authoritative Word*. Ed. Miller.

Moltmann, Jürgen. *Theology of Hope*. Trans. James Leitch. New York: Harper and Row, 1975.

Montgomery, John Warwick. "The Approach of New Shape Roman Catholicism to Scriptural Inerrancy: A Case Study." *God's Inerrant Word*. Ed. Montgomery.

————. "Biblical Inerrancy: What Is at Stake?" *God's Inerrant Word*. Ed. Montgomery.

————. ed. *God's Inerrant Word: An International Symposium On the Trustworthiness of Scripture*. Minneapolis: Bethany, 1974.

————. "Lessons from Luther on the Inerrancy of Holy Writ." *God's Inerrant Word*. Ed. Montgomery.

Moran, Gabriel. "The God of Revelation." *Commonweal* 85 (1967): 499–503.

————. *Scripture and Tradition*. New York: Herder, 1963.

————. *Theology of Revelation*. New York: Herder, 1966.

————. "What Is Revelation?" *Theological Studies* 25 (1964): 217–231.

Muilenburg, James. "The Interpretation of the Bible." *Biblical Authority for Today: Symposium*. Eds. Richardson and W. Schweitzer.

Murray, John. "The Attestation of Scripture." *Infallible Word*. Eds. Stonehouse and Woolley.

Nagy, Barnabas. "A Reformed Contribution." Trans. Dorothy Barton. *Biblical Authority for Today: Symposium*. Eds. Richardson and W. Schweitzer.

Neil, William "The Criticism and Theological Use of the Bible, 1700–1950." *Cambridge History of the Bible,* Vol. 3.

Newman, John Henry. *On the Inspiration of Scripture*. Eds. Derek Holmes and Robert Murray. Washington: Corpus, 1966.

Nicole, Roger. "The Nature of Inerrancy." *Inerrancy and Common Sense*. Eds. Nicole and Michaels.

————, and Michaels, Ramsey, eds. *Inerrancy and Common Sense*. Grand Rapids: Baker, 1980.

Nineham, Dennis. "The Use of the Bible in Modern Theology." *Bulletin of the John Rylands Library* 52 (1969).

————. "Wherein Lies the Authority of the Bible?" *Some Recent Studies*.

On the Authority of the Bible: Some Recent Studies. London: SPCK, 1960.

Orr, James. *Revelation and Inspiration*. Grand Rapids: Eerdmans, 1952.

Outler, Albert. "Scripture, Tradition and Ecumenism." *Scripture and Ecumenism*. Ed. Swidler.

Pache, Rene. *The Inspiration and Authority of Scripture*. Trans. Helen Needham. Chicago: Moody, 1969.

Packer, James. "Calvin's View of Scripture." *God's Inerrant Word*. Ed. Montgomery.

————. "Infallible Scripture and the Role of Hermeneutics." *Scripture and Truth*. Eds. Carson and Woodbridge.

————. " 'Sola Scriptura' in History and Today." *God's Inerrant Word*. Ed. Montgomery.

Palmer, Earl. "The Pastor as a Biblical Christian." *Biblical Authority*. Ed. Rogers.

Pannenberg, Wolfhart. "Die Aufnahme des philosophischen Gottes begriffes als dogmatisches Problem der frühchristlichen Theologie." *Zeitschrift für Kirchengeschichte* 70 (1959): 1–45.

————. "Dogmatic Theses on the Doctrine of Revelation." *Revelation as History*. Ed. Pannenberg.

————. "Heilsgeschehen und Geschichte." *Kerygma und Dogma* 5 (1959): 218–237, 259–288.

————. "Hermeneutics and Universal History." Trans. Paul Achtemeier. *History and Hermeneutic*. Eds. Funk and Ebeling.

————, ed. *Revelation as History*. Trans. David Granskou. New York: Macmillan, 1968.

Piepkorn, Arthur Carl. "What Does 'Inerrancy' Mean?" *Concordia Theological Monthly* 36 (1965): 577–593.

Pinnock, Clark. *Biblical Revelation—The Foundation of Christian Theology*. Chicago: Moody, 1971.

————. "The Inspiration of Scripture and the Authority of Jesus Christ." *God's Inerrant Word*. Ed. Montgomery.

————. "Limited Inerrancy: A Critical Appraisal and Constructive Alternative." *God's Inerrant Word*. Ed. Montgomery.

————. "Three Views of the Bible in Contemporary Theology." *Biblical Authority*. Ed. Rogers.

Pirot, Jean. "Inspiration." *Guide to the Bible: An Introduction to the Study of Holy Scripture*. 2 vols. Eds. Andre Robert and Alphonse Tricot. Trans. Edward Arbez and Martin McGuire. Rome: Desclee, 1951.

Prenter, Regin. "A Lutheran Contribution." *Biblical Authority for Today: Symposium*. Eds. Richardson and W. Schweitzer.

Preus, Robert. *The Inspiration of Scripture: A Study of the Theology of the Seventeenth Century Lutheran Dogmaticians*. London: Oliver and Boyd, 1957.

————. "The View of the Bible Held by the Church: The Early Church Through Luther." *Inerrancy*. Ed. Geisler.

von Rad, Gerhard. "The Form Critical Problem of the Hexateuch." *The*

Problem of the Hexateuch and Other Essays. Trans. Trueman Dicken. New York: McGraw-Hill, 1966.

———. *God at Work in Israel.* Trans. John Marks. Nashville: Abingdon, 1980.

———. *Message of the Prophets.* Trans. David Stalker. New York: Harper and Row, 1967.

———. *Old Testament Theology.* 2 vols. Trans. David Stalker. New York: Harper and Row, 1962.

Rahner, Karl. "Ecriture et Tradition a propose du scheme conciliare sur la revelation divine." *L'homme devant Dieu.*

———. "Exegesis and Dogmatic Theology." *Dogmatic vs. Biblical Theology.* Ed. Herbert Vorgrimler. Baltimore: Helicon, 1964.

———. *Foundations of Christian Faith.* Trans. William Dych. New York: Seabury, 1978.

———. *Inspiration in the Bible.* 2nd rev. ed. Trans. Charles Henkey. Quaestiones Disputatae, Vol. 1. New York: Herder and Herder, 1964.

———. *Theological Investigations.* Vol. 6: *Concerning Vatican II.* Trans. Karl H. and Boniface Kruger. Baltimore: Helicon, 1969.

———. "Über die Schriftinspiratione." *Zeitschrift für Katholische Theologie* 78 (1956): 137–168.

———, and Ratzinger, Joseph. *Revelation and Tradition.* Trans. W.J. O'Hara. Quaestiones Disputatae, Vol. 17. New York: Herder and Herder, 1966.

Ramm, Bernard. "Is 'Scripture Alone' the Essence of Christianity?" *Biblical Authority.* Ed. Rogers.

Rauschenbusch, Walter. *A Theology for the Social Gospel.* Nashville: Abingdon, 1945.

Rees, Paul. "Embattlement or Understanding?" *Biblical Authority.* Ed. Rogers.

Reid, John Kelman Sutherland. *The Authority of Scripture: A Study of the Reformation and Post-Reformation Understanding of the Bible.* London: Methuen, 1962.

Rendtorff, Rolf. *Das Alte Testament: Eine Einführung.* Neukirchen-Vluyn: Neukirchener, 1983.

———. "Hermeneutik des Alten Testaments als Frage nach der Geschichte." *Zeitschrift für Theologie und Kirche* 57 (1960): 27–40.

————. "The Concept of Revelation in Ancient Israel." *Revelation as History*. Ed. Pannenberg.

————, and Koch, Klaus, eds. *Studien zur Theologie der alttestamentlichen Überlieferungen: Gerhard von Rad zum 60. Geburtstag.* Neukirchen: Moers, 1961.

Rendtorff, Trutz. "The Problem of Revelation in the Concept of the Church." *Revelation as History*. Ed. Pannenberg.

Richardson, Alan. "An Anglican Contribution." *Biblical Authority for Today: Symposium*. Eds. Richardson and W. Schweitzer.

————. *The Bible in the Age of Science*. Philadelphia: Westminster, 1961.

————. "The Rise of Modern Biblical Scholarship and Recent Discussion of the Authority of the Bible." *Cambridge History of the Bible,* Vol. 3.

————, and Schweitzer, Wolfgang, eds. *Biblical Authority for Today: A World Council of Churches Symposium on the Biblical Authority for the Churches' Social and Political Message Today*. London: SCM, 1951.

Ridderbos, Herman. "The Inspiration and Authority of Holy Scripture." *Studies in Scripture and Its Authority*. Grand Rapids: Eerdmans, 1978.

Ritschl, Albrecht. *Three Essays*. Trans. Philip Hefner. Philadelphia: Fortress, 1972.

Rogers, Jack, ed. *Biblical Authority*. Waco, Texas: Word, 1977.

————. "The Church Doctrine of Biblical Authority." *Biblical Authority*. Ed. Rogers.

————, and McKim, Donald. *The Authority and Interpretation of the Bible: An Historical Approach*. New York: Harper and Row, 1979.

Rössler, Dietrich. *Gesetz und Geschichte*. Wissenschaftliche Monographien zum Alten und Neuen Testament, Vol. 3. Neukirchen: Moers, 1960.

Runia, Klaas. *Karl Barth's Doctrine of Holy Scripture*. Grand Rapids: Eerdmans, 1962.

Sanday, William. *Inspiration: Eight Lectures on the Early History and Origin of the Doctrine of Biblical Inspiration*. 3rd ed. Bampton Lectures for 1893. London: Longmans, Green, and Company, 1896.

Sanders, James. "Adaptable for Life: The Nature and Function of Canon." *Magnalia Dei: The Mighty Acts of God.* Eds. Frank Cross, Walter Lemke, and Patrick Miller. Garden City: Doubleday, 1976.

———. *Torah and Canon.* Philadelphia: Fortress, 1972.

Schelke, Karl *Die Petrusbriefe.* Herders Theologische Kommentar zum Neuen Testament, Vol. 12, pt. 2. Basle: Herder, 1961.

Schleiermacher, Friedrich Ernst. *The Christian Faith.* 2 vols. Ed. Hugh Ross MacKintosh and James Stewart. New York: Harper and Row, 1963.

Schweitzer, Albert. *The Quest for the Historical Jesus.* Trans. W. Montgomery. New York: Macmillan, 1968.

Schweitzer, Wolfgang. "Biblical Theology and Ethics Today." Trans. John Reid. *Biblical Authority for Today: Symposium.* Eds. Richardson and W. Schweitzer.

Scott, Robert. *Relevance of the Prophets.* New York: Macmillan, 1968.

Scullion, John. *The Theology of Inspiration.* Theology Today, Vol. 10. Ed. Edward Yarnold. Notre Dame: Fides, 1970.

Skilton, John. "The Transmission of the Scriptures." *Infallible Word.* Eds. Stonehouse and Woolley.

Smart, James. *The Interpretation of Scripture.* Philadelphia: Westminster, 1961.

Smith, Richard. "Inspiration and Inerrancy." *Jerome Biblical Commentary.* Eds. Brown, Fitzmyer, and Murphy.

Snaith, Norman. *The Inspiration and Authority of the Bible.* London: Epworth, 1956.

Sproul, Robert. "The Case for Inerrancy: A Methodological Analysis." *God's Inerrant Word.* Ed. Montgomery.

———. "Sola Scriptura: Crucial to Evangelism." *Foundations of Biblical Authority.* Ed. Boice.

Steiger, Lothar. "Revelation-History and Theological Reason: A Critique of the Theology of Wolfhart Pannenberg." *History and Hermeneutic.* Eds. Funk and Ebeling.

Stendahl, Krister. "Ancient Scripture in the Modern World." *Scripture in the Jewish and Christian Traditions.* Ed. Greenspahn.

Stonehouse, Ned Bernard "The Authority of the New Testament." *Infallible Word.* Eds. Stonehouse and Woolley.

————, and Woolley, Paul, eds. *The Infallible Word*. Philadelphia: Presbyterian Guardian, 1946.

Sundberg, Albert. "The Bible Canon and the Christian Doctrine of Inspiration." *Interpretation* 29 (1975): 358–371.

————. "Canon of the New Testament." *Interpreter's Dictionary of the Bible: Supplementary Volume*. Ed. Crim.

————. "Canon Muratori: A Fourth-Century List." *Harvard Theological Review* 66 (1973): 1–41.

————. "The Making of the New Testament Canon." *The Interpreter's One Volume Commentary on the Bible*. Ed. Charles Laymon. Nashville: Abingdon, 1971.

————. "Muratorian Fragment(s)." *Interpreter's Dictionary of the Bible: Supplementary Volume*. Ed. Crim.

————. "The 'Old Testament': A Christian Canon." *Catholic Biblical Quarterly* 30 (1968): 143–155.

————. "The Old Testament of the Early Church." *Harvard Theological Review* 51 (1959): 205–226.

————. *The Old Testament of the Early Church*. Harvard Theological Studies, Vol. 20. Cambridge: Harvard, 1964.

————. "The Protestant Old Testament Canon: Should It Be Re-examined?" *Catholic Biblical Quarterly* 28 (1966): 194–203.

————. "Toward a Revised History of the New Testament Canon." *Studia Evangelica* 4 (1968): 452–461.

Swidler, Leonard, ed. *Scripture and Ecumenism*. Duquesne Studies, Theological Studies, Vol. 3. Pittsburgh: Duquesne, 1965.

Synave, Paul, and Benoit, Pierre. *Prophecy and Inspiration*. Trans. Avery Dulles and Thomas Sheridan. Paris: Desclee, 1961.

Tavard, George. "The Authority of Scripture and Tradition." *Problems of Authority*. Ed. John Todd. Baltimore: Helicon, 1962.

————. "Tradition in Theology: A Problematic Approach." *Perspectives on Scripture and Tradition*. Ed. Kelly.

Thornton, Lionel. *The Form of the Servant*. Vol. 1: *Revelation and the Modern World*. London: Dacre, 1950.

Topel, John. "Rahner and McKenzie on the Social Theory of Inspiration." *Scripture* 16 (1964): 33–44.

Troelsch, Ernst. *The Social Teachings of the Christian Churches*. 2 vols. Trans. Olive Wyon. Chicago: University of Chicago Press, 1960.

Turretin, Francis. *The Doctrine of Scripture.* Ed. John Beardslee, III. Grand Rapids: Baker, 1981.

Turro, James, and Brown, Raymond. "Canonicity." *Jerome Biblical Commentary.* Eds. Brown, Fitzmyer, and Murphy.

Vawter, Bruce. "The Bible in the Roman Catholic Church." *Scripture in Jewish and Christian Traditions,* Ed. Greenspahn.

————. *Biblical Inspiration. Theological Resources.* Philadelphia: Westminster, 1972.

Vischer, Wilhelm. *The Witness of the Old Testament to Christ.* 2 vols. London: Lutterworth, 1949.

Warfield, Benjamin Breckenridge. *The Inspiration and Authority of the Bible.* Ed. Samuel Craig. Philadelphia: Presbyterian and Reformed, 1970.

Weiss, Johannes. *Jesus' Proclamation of the Kingdom of God.* Trans. Richard Hyde Hiers and David Larrimore Holland. Philadelphia: Fortress, 1971.

Wenham, John. "Christ's View of Scripture." *Inerrancy.* Ed. Geisler.

Westermann, Claus. *Basic Forms of Prophetic Speech.* Trans. Hugh White. Philadelphia: Westminster, 1967.

Wiles, Maurice, "Origin as Biblical Scholar." *Cambridge History of the Bible,* Vol. 1.

Wilkens, Ulrich. "Die Bekehrung des Paulus als religionsgeschichtliche Problem." *Zeitschrift für Theologie und Kirche* 56 (1959): 273–293.

————. *Die Missionsreden der Apostelgeschichte.* Wissenschaftliche Mongraphien zum Alten und Neuen Testament, Vol. 5. Neukirchen: Moers, 1961.

————. "The Understanding of Revelation Within the History of Primitive Christianity." *Revelation as History.* Ed. Pannenberg.

Woodbridge, John, and Balmer, Randall. "The Princetonians and Biblical Authority: An Assessment of the Ernest Sandeen Proposal." *Scripture and Truth.* Eds. Carson and Woodbridge.

Wright, George Ernest. "From the Bible to the Modern World." *Biblical Authority for Today: Symposium.* Eds. Richardson and W. Schweitzer.

————. *God Who Acts: Biblical Theology as Recital.* Studies in Biblical Theology, Vol. 8. London: SCM, 1952.

————, and Fuller, Reginald. *The Book of the Acts of God*. Christian Faith Series. Garden City: Doubleday, 1957.

————. "The Authority of the Old Testament." *Infallible Word*. Eds. Stonehouse and Woolley.

Young, Edward. *Thy Word Is Truth*. Grand Rapids: Eerdmans, 1957.

INDEX